The Development of Natural Language Processing

The Development of Natural Language Processing

Research on the Development of Electronic
Information Engineering Technology in China

Chinese Academy of Engineering
Center for Electronics and Information Studies
Chinese Academy of Engineering
Wuhan, Hubei, China

ISBN 978-981-16-1985-4   ISBN 978-981-16-1986-1   (eBook)
https://doi.org/10.1007/978-981-16-1986-1

This Springer imprint is published by the registered company Springer Nature Singapore Pte Ltd.
The registered company address is: 152 Beach Road, #21-01/04 Gateway East, Singapore 189721,
Singapore

Preface

The "Research on the Development of Electronic Information Engineering Technology in China" Book Series

In today's world, the wave of information technologies featured by digitalization, networking, and intelligence is gaining momentum. Information technoslogies are experiencing rapid changes with each passing day and are fully applied in production and life, bringing about profound changes in global economic, political, and security landscapes. Among diverse information technologies, electronic information engineering technology is one of the most innovative and widely used technologies and plays its greatest role in driving the development of other S&T fields. It is not only a field of intense competition in technological innovation, but also an important strategic direction for key players to fuel economic growth and seek competitive advantages over other players. Electronic information engineering technology is a typical "enabling technology" that enables technological progress in almost all other fields. Its integration with biotechnology, new energy technology, and new material technology is expected to set off a new round of technological revolution and industrial transformation, thereby bringing about new opportunities for the evolution of human society. Electronic information is a typical "engineering technology" and one of the most straightforward and practical tools. It realizes direct and close integration of scientific discoveries and technological innovations with industrial developments, greatly speeding up technological progress. Hence, it is regarded as a powerful force to change the world. Electronic information engineering technology is a vital driving force of China's rapid economic and social development in the past seven decades, especially in the past four decades of reform and opening up. Looking ahead, advances and innovations in electronic information engineering technology will remain to be one of the most important engines driving human progress.

CAE is China's foremost academic and advisory institution in engineering and technological sciences. Guided by the general development trends of science and technology around the world, CAE is committed to providing scientific, forward-looking, and timely advice for innovation-driven scientific and technological progress from a strategic and long-term perspective. CAE's mission is to function as a national high-end think tank. To fulfill the mission, the Division of Information and Electronics, under the guidance of its Vice President Zuoning Chen, Director Xicheng Lu, and the Standing Committee, mobilized more than 300 academicians and experts to jointly compile the General Section and the Special Themes of this book (hereinafter referred to as the "Blue Book"). The first stage of compilation was headed by Academicians Jiangxing Wu and Manqing Wu (from the end of 2015 to June 2018), and the second one was headed by Academicians Shaohua Yu and Jun Lu (since September 2018). The purposes of compiling the Blue Book are:

By analyzing technological progress and introducing major breakthroughs and marked achievements made in the electronic information field both at home and abroad each year, to provide reference for China's scientific and technical personnel to accurately grasp the development trend of the field and provide support for China's policymakers to formulate related development strategies.

The "Blue Book" is compiled according to the following principles:

1. *Ensure appropriate description of annual increment*: The field of electronic information engineering technology enjoys a broad coverage and high development speed. Thus, the General Section should ensure an appropriate description of the annual increment, which is about the recent progress, new characteristics, and new trends.
2. *Selection of hot points and highlight points*: China's technological development is still at a mixed stage where it needs to assume the role of follower, contender, and leader simultaneously. Hence, the Special Themes should seek to depict the developmental characteristics the industry it focuses on and should center on the "hot points" and "highlight points" along the development journey.
3. *Integration of General Section and Special Themes*: The program consists of two sections: The General Section and the Special Themes. The former adopts a macro perspective to discuss the global and Chinese development of electronic information engineering technology and its outlook; the latter provides detailed descriptions of hot points and highlight points in the 13 subfields.

Application System

8. Underwater acoustic engineering

13. Computer application

| Acquiring Perception | Computation and Control | Cyber Security |

Acquiring Perception

3. Sensing

5. Electromagnetic space

Computation and Control

10. Control

11. Cognition

12. Computer systems and software

Cyber Security

6. Network and communication

7. Cybersecurity

Common Basis

1. Microelectronics and Optoelectronics   2. Optical engineering

4. Measurement, metrology and Instruments

9. Electromagnetic field and electromagnetic environment effect

Classification Diagrams of 13 Subfields of information and electronic engineering technology

The above graphic displays five categories and 13 subcategories or special themes that bear distinct granularity. However, every subfield is closely connected with each other in terms of technological correlations, which allows easier matching with their corresponding disciplines.

Currently, the compilation of the "Blue Book" is still at a trial stage where careless omissions are unavoidable. Hence, we welcome comments and corrections.

"The Development of Natural Language Processing" in "Research on the Development of Electronic Information Engineering Technology in China" Book Series

The world today is undergoing profound and unprecedented changes. Science and technology are rushing into a fast development lane, the world economy has entered a critical period of replacing the traditional growth drivers by new ones, and China's economy has stepped into a phase of high-quality development. In this context, artificial intelligence (AI) has become an important driving force for a new round of scientific and technological revolution and industrial transformation, and AI is deeply integrated with all walks of life to promote the intelligent transformation and upgrading of industries. Therefore, the innovations of AI technologies and the further expansion of application scenarios in breadth and depth are of great importance.

In July 2017, the State Council of China issued the New Generation Artificial Intelligence Development Plan (GF [2017] No. 35), making clear to establish the next-generation AI key generic technology system covering "knowledge computing engine and knowledge service" and "natural language processing," specifically "focusing on the breakthroughs of knowledge processing, deep search, and visual interaction to realize the automatic acquisition of continuously incrementing knowledge; possess capabilities of concept recognition, entity discovery, attribute prediction, knowledge evolution modeling, and relationship mining; and finally form a multisource, multidisciplinary, and multi-data type cross-media knowledge graph with a scale of billions of entities." In addition, GF (2017) No. 35 focuses on "the breakthroughs of grammatical logic, character concept representation, and deep semantic analysis of natural language, to promote effective communication and free interaction between humans and machines, and to realize intelligent understanding and automatic generation of natural language in multiple styles, multiple languages, and multiple fields."

Language is one of the most fundamental characteristics that distinguish humans from other creatures. It is the carrier of human thoughts and a tool for communication. Knowledge is the result of human understanding of the world in practice and the crystallization of human wisdom. Language is the vehicle for preserving and passing on knowledge. From Jiahu symbols more than 7000 years ago to Internet text today, language and knowledge have always played an important role in human progress.

Natural language expressions are flexible and ambiguous, making it difficult to analyze the structure of language and understand the semantics. There is a huge challenge for machines to acquire and apply large-scale knowledge since the data are complex and heterogeneous, and the knowledge is of diverse forms. Therefore, natural language processing technology that studies how to enable computers to master knowledge, and comprehend and utilize language, is essential to the further development of artificial intelligence.

The research objects of natural language processing are evolved from words, phrases, and sentences to text, and research directions are from language analysis, language understanding, language generation, knowledge graphs, machine translation, to deep semantic understanding, and beyond. This is in line with the development trend of applications. Taking search as an example, keyword-based search was carried out in the early stage. Later, with the popularity of mobile smart terminals, people began to speak directly to mobile phones to search. The newly emerged news feed requires machines to understand users and text content, so as to recommend suitable information to users. And for another typical NLP application machine translation, from text translation, to voice and image translation, now simultaneous interpretation, progress of technology makes the application of machine translation deeper and wider into diverse industries.

In recent years, as AI applications have gradually expanded to all walks of life, application scenarios contain various modal information and have become more complex and diverse. As a result, the research objects of natural language processing have also expanded from language to speech and vision, leading to a new direction of cross-modal semantic understanding. Natural language processing has formed a complete technical system and promoted the development and integration of various technologies.

In the process of technological development and innovation breakthroughs, the boundary of industrial applications continues to expand, from search engines, machine translation, intelligent map, and news feed, to smart hardware and other products. Through the open-source models and open platform, natural language processing technologies are widely used in a variety of industries including finance, medical care, education, energy, and others, to provide a full range of intelligent services and to accelerate the intelligent upgrading of the industry.

In order to better facilitate the development of natural language processing and push for the continuous progress of artificial intelligence, it is a necessity to have full cooperation between the academic and industrial circles, to continue to make breakthroughs and innovations, and make greater contributions to industrial intelligent upgrading and high-quality social and economic development.

This Blue Book focuses on the development of natural language processing. Global trends, natural language processing development status in China, and the future and discussion are presented in four chapters in this book.

Wuhan, China   Chinese Academy of Engineering

List of Series Contributors

The guidance group and working group of *"Research on the Development of Electronic Information Engineering Technology in China"* series are shown as below:

Guidance Group

Leader: Zuoning Chen, Xichen Lu
Member (In alphabetical order):

Aiguo Fei, Baoyan Duan, Binxing Fang, Bohu Li, Changxiang Shen, Cheng Wu, Chengjun Wang, Chun Chen, Desen Yang, Dianyuan Fang, Endong Wang, Guangjun Zhang, Guangnan Ni, Guofan Jin, Guojie Li, Hao Dai, Hequan Wu, Huilin Jiang, Huixing Gong, Jiangxing Wu, Jianping Wu, Jiaxiong Fang, Jie Chen, Jiubin Tan, Jun Lu, Lianghui Chen, Manqing Wu, Qinping Zhao, Qionghai Dai, Shanghe Liu, Shaohua Yu, Tianchu Li, Tianran Wang, Tianyou Chai, Wen Gao, Wenhua Ding, Yu Wei, Yuanliang Ma, Yueguang Lv, Yueming Li, Zejin Liu, Zhijie Chen, Zhonghan Deng, Zhongqi Gao, Zishen Zhao, Zuyan Xu

Working Group

Leader: Shaohua Yu, Jun Lu
Deputy Leader: Da An, Meimei Dang, Shouren Xu
Member (In alphabetical order):

Denian Shi, Dingyi Zhang, Fangfang Dai, Fei Dai, Fei Xing, Feng Zhou, Gang Qiao, Lan Zhou, Li Tao, Liang Chen, Lun Li, Mo Liu, Nan Meng, Peng Wang, Qiang Fu, Qingguo Wang, Rui Zhang, Shaohui Li, Wei He, Wei Xie, Xiangyang Ji, Xiaofeng Hu, Xingquan Zhang, Xiumei Shao, Yan Lu, Ying Wu, Yue Lu, Yunfeng Wei, Yuxiang Shu, Zheng Zheng, Zhigang Shang, Zhuang Liu

Acknowledgements

In the writing of this book, Dr. Wu Hua, Dr. Lv Yajuan, Tian Hao, Sun Yu, Liu Jing, Xiao Xinyan, Dr. Liu Zhanyi, Dr. Guo Yuqing, Wu Tian, Liu Xuan, Zhang Yifei, and others provided great support for information collection and writing. Baidu NLP Department, KG Department, Baidu Research and National Engineering Laboratory for Deep Learning Technology and Applications have done a lot of work. Their forward-looking and innovative research and industrial practices, as well as a large number of industry solutions accumulated in the process, are of great help to the conception and writing of this book. We would like to express our heartfelt thanks here.

Contents

About the Authors

Chinese Academy of Engineering (CAE) is China's foremost academic and advisory institution in engineering and technological sciences, which has been enrolled in the first batch of pilot national high-end think tanks. As a national institution, CAE's missions are to study major strategic issues in economic and social development as well as in engineering technology progress and to build itself into an S&T think tank having significant influences on decision-making of national strategic issues. In today's world, the wave of information technologies featured by digitalization, networking, and intelligence is gaining momentum. Information technologies are experiencing rapid changes with each passing day and are fully applied in production and life, bringing about profound changes in global economic, political, and security landscapes. Among diverse information technologies, electronic information engineering technology is one of the most innovative and widely used technologies and plays its greatest role in driving the development of other S&T fields. In order to better carry out strategic studies on electronic information engineering technology, promote innovation in relevant systems and mechanisms, and integrate superior resources, China Research Center for Electronics and Information Strategies (hereinafter referred to the "Center") was established in November 2015 by CAE in collaboration with Cyberspace Administration of China (CAC), the Ministry of Industry and Information Technology (MIIT), and China Electronics Technology Group Corporation (CETC).

The Center pursues high-level, open, and prospective development and is committed to conducting theoretical and application-oriented researches on crosscutting, overarching, and strategically important hot topics concerning electronic information engineering technologies and providing consultancy services for policymaking by brainstorming ideas from CAE academicians and experts and scholars from national ministries and commissions, businesses, public institutions, universities, and research institutions. The Center's mission is to build a top-notch strategic think tank that provides scientific, forward-looking, and timely advice for national policymaking in terms of electronic information engineering technology.

The main authors of *The Development of Natural Language Processing* are Haifeng Wang and Shaohua Yu.

Haifeng Wang is the first Chinese president in the history of ACL (Association for Computational Linguistics), the most influential international academic organization in the field of natural language processing, and the only ACL member from mainland China. In July 2018, he became the founding chairman of AACL of ACL Asia Pacific branch. He also holds various positions in a number of international academic organizations, international conferences, and international journals. He is the president and director of National Engineering Laboratory of deep learning technology and application. At the same time, he also served as vice president of China artificial intelligence industry development alliance, new generation artificial intelligence industry technology innovation strategy alliance, National Engineering Laboratory for brain-like intelligence technology and application, China Electronics Society, Chinese information society, and other institutions, vice director of Technical Committee of National Engineering Laboratory for big data system software, and member of new generation artificial intelligence strategy advisory committee.

Shaohua Yu Academician of Chinese Academy of Engineering(CAE), is an information and communication network technology expert. He is the chief engineer of China Information and Communication Technologies Group Co., Ltd., the director of State Key Laboratory of Optical Communication Technologies and Network, the vice president of China Institute of Communications, the member of national 863 Program Network and communication subject expert group, the member of cyber power strategy research advisory group, and the national integrated circuit industry development advisory committee Member. He has been engaged in the research of optical fiber communication and network technology for a long time, presided over and completed more than ten national projects such as 973 and 863, all of which have achieved transformation of achievements and a large number of applications. It is one of the pioneers of the integration of SDH (Synchronous Digital Hierarchy) and Internet (including Ethernet).

Chapter 1
Global Trends

Language is the method of communication and the carrier of human thoughts and knowledge. It fully expresses both human emotions and cognitions. Language implies a large amount of knowledge that mankind has continuously learned about the world in practice, and it is one of the important signs of human intelligence.

In computer science, distinguished from well-formed artificial languages (such as programming languages), the languages used in human daily life are called natural languages. The theories and methods that study the use of computers to learn and utilize knowledge and language are collectively referred to as natural language processing (NLP). The study of NLP is closely related to artificial intelligence since its inception. In 1950, Alan Turing introduced the famous Turing test in which a machine carried on a conversation with people in natural language, and its ability to exhibit behavior indistinguishable from that of a human was regarded as a criterion for judging whether the machine has intelligence.

According to contemporary linguistic theories, natural language mainly involves five levels of analysis: symbol, morphology, syntax, semantics and pragmatics. Correspondingly, there is the same hierarchy of essential NLP technologies. Symbolic techniques mainly refer to the input methods of characters and phonetics, etc. Lexical analysis includes word segmentation, stemming, part-of-speech (POS) tagging, named entity recognition (NER), and more. Syntactic analysis consists of chunking, constituency parsing, dependency parsing, and more. Semantics traditionally contains semantic role labeling (SRL), anaphora resolution, semantic representation and the like, and pragmatics research on the interrelationship between language components and context, between literal meaning and internal meaning. These basic technologies lay the foundation for the research and development of high-level NLP applications, such as machine translation, information retrieval, human-machine dialogue, automatic question answering, information recommendation and filtering, text summarization and generation, among others.

Chinese Academy of Engineering, *The Development of Natural Language Processing*, https://doi.org/10.1007/978-981-16-1986-1_1

1.1   History of Natural Language Processing

In the history of NLP technology evolution, we witness two main trends originating from their philosophical tradition: rationalism and empiricism. Since the late 1940s, proposals and explorations of machine translation (MT) and human-machine dialogue systems have given rise to NLP technologies. In the following decades, rationalism and empiricism successively dominated the field of NLP, promoting constant development along two different technical routes. From the 1960s to the 1980s, the mainstream trend is rule-based rationalism or symbolic NLP, during which a great number of expert systems were produced. Up to the 1990s, there was a revolution in the NLP field with the prevalence of statistical machine learning algorithms, and NLP technologies have made great progress driven by increasing popularity of the Internet. Around 2010, there was a renewed interest in connectionism, a branch of empiricism, which models cognitive activities by simulating biological brains using artificial neural networks (ANN). ANNs have further evolved into the more sophisticated deep neural networks (DNN) that have tremendously advanced the state of the art of computer vision (CV), speech, and NLP fields, kicking off the new era of AI.

1.1.1   The Early Stage

"To build the tower of Babel confounded human language, since then translators became a necessity." (Ma Zuyi, A Brief History of Chinese Translation, p. 1) As early as the beginning of the world, humans had the need to translate languages to understand each other. In 1946, the unveiling of the first electronic digital computer ENIAC provided the hardware prerequisite for the use of a computer to translate and process languages. The idea of using computers for translation of natural languages was first proposed by Warren Weaver in 1947 and later elaborated on in the "Translation" Memorandum. In 1954, Georgetown University cooperated with IBM to carry out the first public demonstration of a Russian-English machine translation system on an IBM-701 computer, by which more than 60 Russian sentences were fully automatically translated into English with 6 grammar rules and a lexicon consisting of 250 vocabularies. The Georgetown-IBM experiment is the first MT debut in history, anchoring the start of MT that has stepped from vision into reality. It is plausible to say that the demand for machine translation has given the birth to NLP.

In addition to the exploration of machine translation, the development of linguistics, mathematics, and computer science during this period also laid theoretical foundations for NLP technology. In 1951, in investigation of McCulloch-Pitts neural nets, American mathematician Stephen Cole Kleene introduced the notion of regular expressions and finite automata, by which a valid regular language can be recognized. In 1956, American linguist Noam Chomsky published *Three Models for the*

Description of Language, putting forward the classical formulation known as Chomsky Hierarchy in which languages are classified into four types based on the expressive power of their generative grammar. He proved that there was an equivalence relation between formal grammars and automata by which the languages generated and the languages recognized constituted the same class. These works illustrated mathematic properties of formal languages, making a major fundamental contribution to formal language theory. In those same years, Claude Shannon, the father of information theory, applied statistical model of the Markov chain to describe language with an automaton and migrated the concept of entropy in thermodynamics to measure the information of language like English, i.e. quantifying information entropy based on statistics of English. Their work paved the way for research splitting into rationalism and empiricism, while both having substantial impact on the evolution of NLP technologies.

The Dartmouth Conference of 1956 officially proposed the concept of Artificial Intelligence, and thereafter natural language processing has become an indispensable part of it. As a measure of machine intelligence, human-machine dialogue system became a major focus of research at that time. In 1966, Joseph Weizenbaum of the MIT AI Laboratory published the world's first chatterbot program called ELIZA, which could simulate a psychotherapist to carry out conversations with a patient. ELIZA simulated conversation simply by using pattern matching and substitution methodology without any idea of knowing what it was talking about, yet ELIZA sometimes provided a startlingly human-like response that many users were convinced of its intelligence at that time. The technique of handcrafted patterns has also instructive significance for subsequent formal knowledge representation and has always been used in practical dialogue systems for its simple, easy, and efficient characteristics. For example, the chat robot ALICE [1], winner of the Turing test Loebner Prize competition in 2000, 2001, and 2004, also uses a pattern matching method to retrieve answers, whereas it is equipped with a knowledge base containing more than 40,000 templates, far larger than 200 that Eliza equipped.

Despite intense research efforts being made, the early MT and dialogue systems are more or less toy systems, still far from practical usage. In November 1966, the U.S. Automatic Language Processing Advisory Committee (ALPAC) issued a report, Language and Machines, claiming that machine translation is slower, less accurate, and more expensive than human translation, hence completely denying the feasibility of machine translation. Since then, little further research in MT was conducted and NLP fell out of favor.

1.1.2 The Golden Years of Heuristics and Expert Systems

The early development of NLP technology was oriented towards the realization of AI. On one hand, it continued in the direction of human-machine dialogue systems. On the other hand, it was deeply influenced by proving theorems with machines,

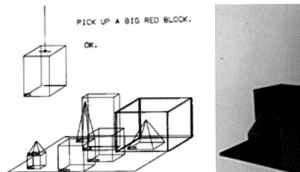
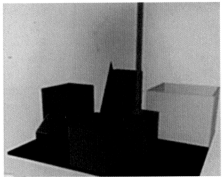

Fig. 1.1 The Winograd's "blocks worlds." The original screen display (left). The later color 3D rendering by University of Utah (right)

wherein the symbolic school based on logical reasoning and formal expression was the mainstream.

In 1968–1970, Terry Winogard, a Ph.D. student at MIT, developed a natural language system SHRDLU [2] for a specific scenario. This is a virtual "blocks worlds" shown on a display screen, in which people use limited vocabulary and grammar to order a robotic hand with visual functions to manipulate the building blocks, such as picking up a specific block (color, shape, size) to place atop another one (Fig. 1.1). SHRDLU understood and executed instructions based on Chomsky's transformational generative grammar. If it could not understand the command, it would ask questions to make it clear. SHRDLU integrated many technologies including natural language input, output, understanding, generation, knowledge representation, and planning. It was more complex than ELIZA and had more profound academic significance. In 2017, Fei-fei Li's team from Stanford University and researchers from Facebook built a similar data set, CLEVR [3], for research on visual question answering and reasoning.

In this period, the AI field was committed to transforming human expert knowledge into a formal knowledge base and realized intelligence through the mechanism of inference engine based on knowledge. These types of intelligent systems are called Expert Systems.

In 1968, Edward Feigenbaum, director of Stanford Computation Center, collaborated with the founder of the Department of Genetics and Nobel Prize winner Joshua Lederberg, and chemist Carl Djerassi, to design an expert system called DENDRAL (an acronym of "Dendritic Algorithm") for judging molecular structures of substances. DENDRAL took raw mass spectrometry data of an organic compound as input and generated its possible molecular structure by chemical heuristics as an output. DENDRAL is considered the first expert system. Following the success of DENDRAL, one of the team members, Bruce Buchanan, continued to develop a medical diagnosis system, MYCIN, attempting to identify bacteria causing infections and to recommend antibiotics based on patients' symptoms and medical test results. Although MYCIN was never actually used in practice, it reported an acceptability rating of 69% on treatment plan, which was comparable to or even better than that of general practitioners. More importantly, MYCIN initiated production rules that were later widely adopted by expert systems, and the architecture separating the domain-specific knowledge from inference engine formed the basis for the more general expert system tool E-MYCIN. In 1977, Feigenbaum summarized the efforts at codifying the knowledge for use in expert systems as "knowledge engineering" at the Fifth International Conference on Artificial Intelligence, turning the initial prototypes into a systematic methodology. Expert systems have experienced a golden period of about 20 years. As the theory and technology become more mature, thousands of expert systems have been developed and applied to many fields such as chemistry, biology, medicine, meteorology, geological prospecting, law, and commerce.

The development of expert systems fueled the research of knowledge representation, which was dedicated to representing knowledge using predefined symbols in a data structure that can be utilized by a computer such as expert system. The earliest work in knowledge representation are logics originated from theorem provers. Later efforts of cognitive revolution in psychology led to production systems such as the one featured in the cognitive model developed by Allen Newell and Herbert Simon in 1972. In 1975, Marvin Minsky proposed the Frame Theory, using frames to represent categories describing things in the world. Frames are derived from the philosophical stereotype that assembles facts about particular objects and arranges the object types into a taxonomic hierarchy, which has significant overlap with the later object-oriented programming languages. Semantic network is another knowledge representation formalism that at the same time has equivalent capacity to frame. It is a directed or undirected graph consisting of vertices, which represent objects or concepts, and edges, which represent semantic relations between concepts. Semantic network is regarded as a precursor to the formalism termed as knowledge graph today.

With the development of knowledge engineering, there were attempts to construct large-scale knowledge systems. In 1984, Douglas Lenat, a student of Feigenbaum, started and led the project Cyc. As implied by its name which was derived from "encyclopedia," Cyc was committed to codify, in machine-usable form, all the mundane facts that composed human common sense, which was estimated to require at least 250,000 rules and 350 person-years to build by hand. Lenat predicted at that time that Cyc would be pre-installed in every computer within 15 years. Unfortunately, the project has lasted more than 30 years and has few successful applications so far. Another more practical knowledge system is the WordNet developed by researchers in the Cognitive Science Laboratory of Princeton University under the direction of psychologist George Miller starting in 1985. WordNet is a lexical database grouping all English words into sets of cognitive synonyms (synsets), each expressing a distinct concept. Synsets are interlinked by conceptual-semantic relations including hyponyms, meronyms, antonyms, and more. WordNet has become a de facto NLP tool for English text analysis. As a Chinese analog to WordNet, the Chinese concept knowledge base HowNet had been constructed by Professor Dong Zhendong since 1988. The efforts of HowNet in defining all Chinese words by a set of sememes elaborately designed has continued for nearly 30 years, resulting in a knowledge dictionary containing more than 100,000 concepts, which is of great value to Chinese information processing. Although these hand-crafted knowledge systems are time-consuming, labor-intensive, and limited in scale, they have accumulated invaluable experience and laid a necessary foundation for subsequent large-scale automatic knowledge mining and construction.

During the same period, the research and development of machine translation gradually revived, and a number of translation products based on linguistic rules developed in an engineering approach came into the market. In 1976, University of Montreal cooperated with the Canadian Government Translation Bureau to launch the TAUM-METEO system, which could translate weather forecasts between English and French. In 1978, on the basis of SYSTRAN developed by Georgetown University, the Commission of the European Communities successfully realized machine translation between English, French, German, Spanish, Italian, Portuguese, and other language pairs. With the fifth-generation computer project, many Japanese firms got involved in developing English-Japanese machine translation systems, and a cooperation between Japan and four other Asian countries were carried out on the R&D of multilingual machine translation. In China, Chinasoft Corporation issued the English-Chinese machine translation system TransStar during the Seventh Five-Year Plan period. In 1984, professor Makoto Nagao at Kyoto University proposed a new idea of machine translation using pre-prepared examples for repeated phrases in translation, which is now termed example-based machine translation (EBMT). EBMT neglected syntactic and semantic rules used for decades, and encouraged the further statistical machine translation method.

Nevertheless, in the late 1980s, with the failure of Japan's Fifth-Generation computer project whose ambition was to create a super-computer for knowledge and information processing, the commercial wave of AI subsided, and the NLP development again fell into a bottleneck period.

1.1.3 The Rise of Statistical Machine Learning

Since the 1990s, data and information have explosively increased with the growth of the Internet, and in the meantime computational speed and storage capacity have increased substantially. In these favorable conditions, more interest was shown in machine learning methods based on data statistics. Hidden Markov models (HMMs) and other probability methods have been successfully applied to speech recognition. Under the influence, empiricism gradually gained the upper hand in the NLP field, and data-driven statistical models became widely used in various fundamental and application tasks. For example, HMMs, Maximum Entropy (EM) models, Support Vector Machines (SVM), Conditional Random Fields (CRF), and others are applied to word segmentation, POS tagging, NER, and other tasks. Mutual information, decision trees, and Bayesian classifiers are used in word disambiguation, and

Probabilistic Context-Free Grammar (PCFG) is used in syntactic parsing. N-gram model is adopted to determine the validity of language, and edit distance and Vector Space Model (VSM) are adopted to measure the similarity of two language segments. Topic models such as Probabilistic Latent Semantic Analysis (PLSA) and Latent Dirichlet Allocation (LDA) are applied to text topic analysis, and so on.

In terms of machine translation, Peter Brown and his colleagues at IBM proposed the statistical machine translation (SMT) method based on source-channel model [4] in the early 1990s. They trained on about three million sentence pairs of the Canadian Parliament corpus to implement the first statistical-based machine translation system CANDIDE, marking the birth of SMT. In 1999, a group of researchers gathered at the Summer School of Johns Hopkins University to reproduce IBM's SMT model and developed an open-source toolkit GIZA, which substantially accelerated the SMT improvement. In 2002, Franz Josef Och proposed a new method based on maximum entropy model, expanding the original IBM source-channel model into a more flexible SMT framework that can integrate other knowledge. In 2003, Philipp Koehn at the University of Edinburgh introduced a phrase-based statistical translation model, which significantly improved the SMT performance. In 2005, David Chiang proposed a hierarchical method combining the strength of phrase-based and syntax-based translation, and further progress was made in the translation model. In 2006, Chinese scholar Haifeng Wang proposed a method using Pivot Language to translate between data scares languages [5]. Another important invention to promote the MT development is the automatic evaluation method BLEU (Bilingual Evaluation Understudy), which provides objective evaluation criteria for translation results and avoids the tedious and expensive manual evaluation. In 2006, Google launched its SMT system trained on massive data, which was the first Internet MT service.

NLP applications in this period were mainly driven by the development of the Internet, which became the most important resource for obtaining information. In 1993, a project called Architext was created by six Stanford undergraduates to use word statistics to improve relevancy of searches on the Internet, which eventually evolved into a crawling search engine Excite at the end of 1995. The first popular search engine was YAHOO! launched in 1994, which operated on a human-edited catalog of websites rather than the contents of webpages. In 1998, two Ph.D. students at Stanford University Sergey Brin and Larry Page released the modern search engine Google, which searched webpages by matching keywords to search queries and ranked the search results by the PageRank algorithm. In 2000, Baidu was founded by Robin Li and an independent search engine website was launched in the following year.

On the other hand, with the advantages of statistical machine learning, expert systems have been declining, whereas the need for knowledge representation and large-scale knowledge base construction based on Internet information has become increasingly prominent. In 2001, Tim Berners-Lee, the inventor of the World Wide Web, coined the term Semantic Web and created the semantic markup languages Resource Description Framework (RDF) and Web Ontology Language (OWL) in order to make Internet data machine-readable. These specifications provided a

Fig. 1.2 A search result based on Knowledge Graph

common framework to standardize the earlier relatively free knowledge representations of the semantic network. In 2006, Berners-Lee proposed the principles of Linked Open Data for publishing datasets on the Internet building upon the Semantic Web technologies, which brought out a large number of new-generation knowledge bases, such as DBpedia, Yago, Freebase, and others. In 2011, IBM's question answering system, Watson, defeated human players in the American TV quiz show Jeopardy! to win the championship. The key factor of its victory was the construction of a massive multi-source knowledge base covering information from WordNet, Yago, DBpedia, IMDB (Internet Movie Database), and many other sources, and using open-source search engines to search for possible answers and making comprehensive judgments through a variety of algorithms. In 2010, Google acquired Metaweb, a company that developed Freebase, which powered in part Google's Knowledge Graph. Google officially announced Knowledge Graph in 2012 as a new feature to enhance its search engine results with an additional infobox, which presented in structured data the relevant facts to the user query gathered from Knowledge Graph (Fig. 1.2).

1.1.4 The Heyday Dominated by Deep Learning

Although the earliest research in neural network can be traced back to the 1940s and 1950s, it had not been widely used and developed due to limitations in algorithms, computing power, and data scale at that time. Up to the mid-1980s, the advances in Boltzmann machines, backpropagation algorithms, Convolutional Neural Networks (CNNs), Long Short-Term Memory networks (LSTMs), among others, have driven renewed interest in connectionism and neural works. In 2006, a landmark paper published in *Science* by Geoffrey Hinton and Ruslan Salakhutdinov officially introduced the term of Deep Neural Network. DNN models take as input raw features and are trained in an end-to-end manner obviating human-guided feature engineering that was typically adopted in traditional machine learning. Furthermore, deep learning demonstrates distinctly superior performance against statistical machine learning as the scale of data increases. Since 2010, DNN models have gradually replaced traditional machine learning models, bringing about technological breakthroughs in various disciplines including speech, computer vision, and NLP, and eventually leading to the "big bang" of AI.

Different from symbolic approaches that represent semantics by a combination of explicit symbols such as characters or words, deep learning techniques embed latent syntactic or semantic features of natural language in a distributed representation as dense, low-dimensional, continuous vectors called word embedding. In 2001, a research group at the University of Montreal led by Yoshua Bengio proposed the first neural language model, which yielded word embedding as a by-product of the model's parameters learned in training. In 2013 and 2014, the training tools for word embedding Word2Vec and GloVe have been released successively, making it possible to train word embedding efficiently based on a large-scale corpus. Since then, deep neural network models with pre-trained word embedding have reached the mainstream in NLP.

In 2014, Google launched a sequence-to-sequence translation architecture based on Recurrent Neural Network (RNN). In 2015 and 2016, Baidu, Google, and some others successively released their Neural Machine Translation (NMT) systems based on neural networks. In 2017, the Transformer [6], a CNN translation model based exclusively on attention mechanism, was launched, which outperformed the previous RNN architectures in both aspects of translation quality and speed, promoting the performance of MT systems into a new level. More importantly, models can focus on certain parts of the input sequence according to such simple but powerful attention mechanism, which eventually enhances the ability to capture language properties. Since then, feature extractors based on the Transformer framework have been widely used in many kinds of language modelling tasks.

The year of 2018 anchored a new epoch in the field of NLP. In February, the Allen Institute for AI (AI2) introduced a new type of bidirectional LSTM-based language model ELMo (Embedding from Language Models), which can generate deep contextualized word representations as basic features used for downstream NLP tasks. Subsequently, OpenAI proposed a generative pre-training language model GPT (Generative Pre-Training) based on the Transformer encoder mechanism. At the end of 2018, Google released the bidirectional language model BERT [7] (Bidirectional Encoder Representations from Transformers), a new method of pre-training language representations in a two-step paradigm, where models were first pre-trained on a massive general-purpose corpus and then fine-tuned on target-specific tasks. BERT has given a huge improvement over the state-of-the-art across a wide range of NLP applications. Thereafter, pre-training language model has been consistently improved in training tasks, learning mechanisms, data scale, and other directions. Global high-tech giants such as OpenAI, Facebook, Google, Microsoft, Carnegie Mellon University, Washington University, and others have successively released multi-lingual representation model XLM, auto-regressive pre-training model XLNet, super-scale parameter model RoBERTa, lightweight model ALBert, generation-oriented models GPT-2 and T5, multi-task model MT-DNN, cross-modal models Unicoder-VL and VideoBERT, and many others. In China, Baidu and Tsinghua University respectively proposed their pre-training language representation models enhanced with heterogenous knowledge. Baidu ERNIE (Enhanced Representation from kNowledge IntEgration) [8] greatly improved performance of various NLP tasks. Alibaba released StructBERT, a model that integrated language structure information, and more. With impact of the innovative "pre-training and fine-tuning" paradigm, we have seen progress at unprecedented scale and speed achieved in the field of NLP, which is now stepping into a new stage of industrial production.

1.2 Development of NLP Technology

1.2.1 Recent Boom of NLP

In recent years, driven by the key elements of data, algorithms and computing power, artificial intelligence has entered a period of rapid development. As one of the key general technologies of AI, the NLP field has shown an unprecedented vigorous development trend.

In the field of academic research, NLP technology has become the research focus in recent years. Taking ACL (Annual Conference of the Association for Computational Linguistics), the top international conference in the NLP field, as an example, the number of submitted long papers has steadily increased from 638 in 2010 to 1045 in 2018, surged to 1740 in 2019, and exceeded 2000 in 2020. Given that the acceptance rate has been maintained at 25% over the years, the number of accepted papers has increased from 160 in 2010 to 256 in 2018, 447 in 2019, and exceeded 500 in 2020 [9]. Within just 2 years, the numbers of both submissions and acceptance have doubled (Fig. 1.3).

This trend is also reflected in the number of pre-published papers on arXiv. Since 2010, the number of papers in the AI field has been constantly increasing. By 2019 it has increased by more than 20 times, and the number in the sub-fields of computation and language has even exceeded 60 times [10] (Fig. 1.4).

AI patents, including NLP technologies, are growing more rapidly. According to the World Intellectual Property Organization (WIPO) [11], from 2012 to 2017, the annual growth rate of AI patent applications was 28%, and that of scientific and technological literature was 5.6%. The ratio of scientific and technological papers to patents decreased from 8:1 in 2010 to 3:1 in 2016, indicating that AI technology is shifting from theoretical research to commercialized products and services. By the end of 2016, there were 340,000 AI-related patent applications worldwide, more than half of which were applied after 2013. Among them, 256,456 patents involve AI applied technologies, accounting for approximately 75% of the total number of AI patents. The top three technologies are: computer vision, accounting for 49%; natural language processing, 14%; and speech processing, 13%.

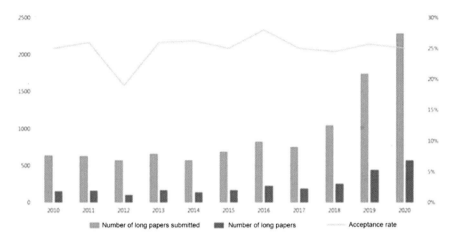

Fig. 1.3   Submission and acceptance of long papers at ACL in 10 years

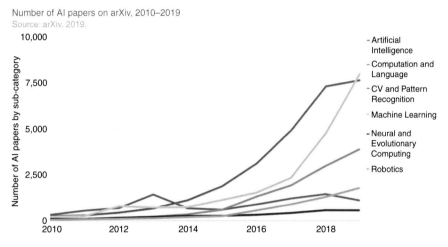

Fig. 1.4   AI paper published on arXiv in recent years

With the prosperity of NLP, more and more people are engaged in study and research in this field. However, there is a shortage of high-end talent that causes increasingly fierce competition. At present, most top NLP talent gathers in the United States, but China has become more and more attractive to talent. Based on the statistical analysis of academic papers and authors collected by AMiner [12], a big data mining and service platform for scientific information, the top scholars in the NLP field are mainly on the east and west coasts of the U.S., Midwestern Europe, and Southeast Asia. The U.S. attracts most of the NLP talent, and also is the country where talent flows quickly. Based on the analysis of the authors of academic conference papers in 2019, 2465 top talents in AI moved into China and 2310 moved out. Among them, 475 moved into China from the U.S., more than the

440 who moved into the U.S. from China. It is clear that China's attraction to top international AI talent keeps increasing (Fig. 1.5).

1.2.2   Characteristics of NLP Technologies

In general, NLP technologies have made significant progress, showing the following characteristics:

1. Massive data and diverse knowledge provide strong support for the rapid development of NLP technologies.

With the birth and rise of the Internet and mobile communication technologies, we have entered the era of big data, wherein the scale of data generated has increased exponentially. According to the forecast of the International Data Corporation (IDC) report [13], the global data sphere will grow from 33 ZB in 2018 to 175 ZB by 2025, with an expected compound annual growth rate (CAGR) of 27% in the next few years (Fig. 1.6).

Data is an important foundation for AI applications including NLP. Whether the early stage domain-specific knowledge was handcrafted by experts, or later regularities were automatically discovered by statistical machine learning methods and were used to analyze and make decisions, all indicate the obvious importance of data. In recent years, GPU (Graphics Processing Unit) and TPU (Tensor Processing Unit) clusters have brought significant improvements in computing power, making it possible that unsupervised and semi-supervised learning methods utilize unlabeled data to train models, further tapping the great potential of big data. Deep neural network modeling can more effectively discover the latent knowledge in large-scale data. With the increasing growth of data scale and model complexity, the performance of various NLP tasks has continued to improve.

In the meanwhile, large-scale datasets are also driving the emergence and development of new research directions. For instance, the release of data sets such as Google's CNN/Daily Mail, Stanford's SQuAD (Stanford Question Answering Dataset), and Microsoft's MS-MARCO (MAchine Reading COmprehension) has accelerated the development of Machine Reading Comprehension (MRC), which has quickly become a popular topic in NLP research. Baidu released DuReader, a large-scale Chinese reading comprehension dataset based on real web texts, and organized relevant competitions, which further promoted the progress and practical process of the MRC technology.

Another subject is to transform data into semantics and knowledge, which is a more basic issue that reflects the value of data, and makes knowledge graphs the most typical representative of contemporary knowledge engineering. The rapid progress and wide application of machine learning, has significantly improved the efficiency of knowledge extraction and large-scale knowledge base construction,

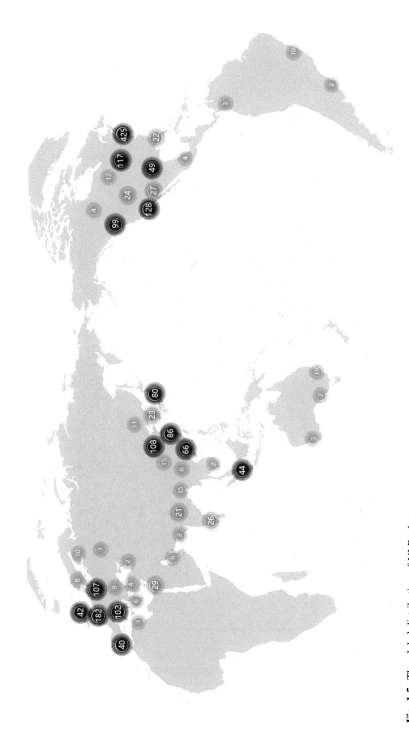

Fig. 1.5 The global distribution of NLP talent

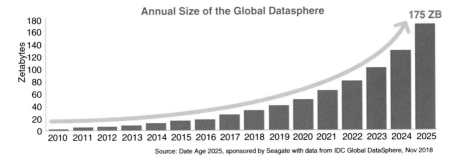

Fig. 1.6 IDC prediction for the global datasphere growth

and has also greatly promoted the application of knowledge in AI tasks such as question answering and recommendation. The knowledge graph technology has formed a relatively complete and mature technical system. More importantly, the construction and application of knowledge has formed a closed loop in the big data environment. On one hand, acquire knowledge from multi-source heterogeneous data on the Internet to construct a large-scale multi-modal knowledge graph, which will be incrementally and automatically updated. On the other hand, explore knowledge to deeply understand multi-modal data including text, speech, image, and video, realize semantic association and fusion between cross-media data, and build a unified knowledge cognitive computing engine with abilities of knowledge evolution modeling, induction, and deduction, to provide intelligent services for the Internet and all walks of life. During this process further knowledge would be obtained. Through this continuous iteration and mutual promotion, the transitions from data to knowledge and from information services to intelligent services would come into reality.

2. The deep learning revolution [14] has become a new driving force to accelerate NLP breakthroughs.

Compared with rule-based symbolic methods or traditional statistical approaches prevailed in early days, the NLP methodologies and paradigms led by deep learning techniques have undergone profound changes.

Deep learning algorithms, especially innovative pre-training language models, makes end-to-end semantic analysis possible. As a result, syntactic analysis, which was once the core task of NLP in the age of formal grammar and statistical machine learning, is fading out. Traditional language analysis methods relying on a pipeline of separate tasks including word segmentation, POS tagging, syntactic parsing, and more, are so complicated that errors are prone to propagate during the process. The end-to-end NLP approaches based on deep learning models directly learn semantic labels from the raw text input, obviating the intermediate steps, which entails substantial simplicity in the architecture and makes great improvements in analysis accuracy. Furthermore, research shows that syntactic and semantic features have been captured in different layers of the language models pre-trained on a massive amount of data, thus there is no need to carry out syntactic parsing to provide explicit syntactic structures for downstream tasks.

Regarding to the scope of text that can be processed, traditional morphology and syntactic analysis are often limited to a single sentence, while the fast-growing MRC technology has broken the limitation of sentence boundaries, making it possible to go from understanding a sentence to a document, and further to text cross-document. This trend has also displayed in text generation, where we see new technologies such as automatic summarization based on multi-document aggregation and event context generation based on multi-document.

In addition, the unified semantic representation based on deep neural networks has significantly improved capabilities of multi-task learning and multi-technique fusion. In the NLP field, the multi-task joint model of word segmentation, POS tagging, and NER consistently improves the accuracy of all the lexical analysis tasks, and the multi-language MT model significantly improves the translation quality of sparse-data languages. Moreover, a large number of new tasks that involve multi-modal information have emerged, such as image caption generation, visual question and answer, visual dialogue, text-based image generation, and more. Some cross-modal tasks such as simultaneous interpretation and human-machine dialogue have also achieved technological breakthroughs. Deep learning technology has made great progress in the fields of speech, CV, NLP, and beyond. From the perspective of the fundamental theory, the boundaries of each field are becoming blurred and deeply intersected. Integration of various techniques will further improve the NLP performance and expand the scope of research and applications of cross-modal semantic understanding.

3. The performance of NLP technologies has been significantly improved, and on some tasks has come close to, reached, and even surpassed human level.

The pre-training and fine-tuning paradigm leads the revolution in NLP technologies, achieves major technological breakthroughs, and greatly improves system performance. Since 2018, the two-step strategy based on general language model pre-training and fine-tuning for specific tasks has almost become the standard configuration of NLP. The massive general corpus thoroughly captures universal language features and provides a solid foundation for NLP tasks to effectively solve the sparse-data problem in specific domains and improve the performance of a diverse range of downstream tasks to a new level.

GLUE, a general language understanding evaluation benchmark that includes nine typical NLP tasks such as sentiment classification, sentence similarity, question answering, and language inference, is one of the most authoritative evaluation sets in the NLP field. The full score of the GLUE benchmark is 100, and the average score performed by humans is 87.1. At the beginning of 2018, when the leaderboard was released, the baseline system score was only 70. In the following 2 years, the leaderboard has been continuously refreshed. By the end of 2019, several semantic understanding systems developed by Baidu, Google, Alibaba, PingAn, and other institutes have successively broken the 90 mark, surpassing human scores (Fig. 1.7).

Rank	Name	Model	URL	Score	CoLA	SST-2	MRPC	STS-B	QQP	MNLI-m	MNLI-mm	QNLI	RTE	WNLI	AX
1	ERNIE Team - Baidu	ERNIE	[link]	90.1	72.2	97.1	93.0/90.7	92.9/92.5	75.2/90.8	91.2	90.6	98.0	90.4	94.5	49.3
2	Microsoft D365 AI & MSR AI & GATECHMT-DNN-SMART		[link]	89.9	69.5	97.5	93.7/91.6	92.9/92.5	73.9/90.2	91.0	90.8	99.2	89.7	94.5	50.2
3	T5 Team - Google	T5	[link]	89.7	70.8	97.1	91.9/89.2	92.5/92.1	74.6/90.4	92.0	91.7	96.7	92.5	93.2	53.1
+ 4	王玥	ALICE v2 large ensemble (Alibaba DAMO NLP)	[link]	89.5	71.3	97.1	93.9/91.9	93.0/92.5	74.8/91.0	90.7	90.4	99.2	87.4	91.8	48.4
5	XLNet Team	XLNet (ensemble)	[link]	89.5	70.2	97.1	92.9/90.5	93.0/92.6	74.7/90.4	90.9	90.9	99.0	88.5	92.5	48.4
6	ALBERT-Team Google Language	ALBERT (Ensemble)	[link]	89.4	69.1	97.1	93.4/91.2	92.5/92.0	74.2/90.5	91.3	91.0	99.2	89.2	91.8	50.2
7	Microsoft D365 AI & UMD	FreeLB-RoBERTa (ensemble)	[link]	88.8	68.0	96.8	93.1/90.8	92.4/92.2	74.8/90.3	91.1	90.7	98.8	88.7	89.0	50.1
8	Facebook AI	RoBERTa	[link]	88.5	67.8	96.7	92.3/89.8	92.2/91.9	74.3/90.2	90.8	90.2	98.9	88.2	89.0	48.7
+ 9	Microsoft D365 AI & MSR AI	MT-DNN-ensemble	[link]	87.6	68.4	96.5	92.7/90.3	91.1/90.7	73.7/89.9	87.9	87.4	96.0	86.3	89.0	42.8
10	GLUE Human Baselines	GLUE Human Baselines	[link]	87.1	66.4	97.8	86.3/80.8	92.7/92.6	59.5/80.4	92.0	92.8	91.2	93.6	95.9	-
11	Stanford Hazy Research	Snorkel MeTaL	[link]	83.2	63.8	96.2	91.5/88.5	90.1/89.7	73.1/89.9	87.6	87.2	93.9	80.9	65.1	39.9
32	GLUE Baselines	BiLSTM+ELMo+Attn	[link]	70.0	33.6	90.4	84.4/78.0	74.2/72.3	63.1/84.3	74.1	74.5	79.8	58.9	65.1	21.7
		BiLSTM+ELMo	[link]	67.7	32.1	89.3	84.7/78.0	70.3/67.8	61.1/82.6	67.2	67.9	75.5	57.4	65.1	21.3

Fig. 1.7 Screenshot of the GLUE Leaderboard on December 11, 2019

NLP technologies are more and more mature, laying the foundation for large-scale production and commercialization.

1.3 Industrial Applications of NLP

From the perspective of technology breakthrough, industrial structure reform, and the latest trend of policy deployment in various countries, AI technologies, including NLP, are accelerating innovations and starting large-scale industrial applications, becoming an important driving force for a new round of scientific and technological revolution and industrial transformation.

1.3.1 Industrial-Scale Production

With the fast development of Internet and information technology, there has been a huge surge in various smart devices and data volumes. Human beings have entered the intelligent era, and the demand for applications related to natural language processing has also grown rapidly, forming an industrial scale. According to data statistics from the market analysis agency Mordor Intelligence [15], in 2019, the global NLP market was 10.9 billion US dollars, and it is expected to grow to 34.8 billion US dollars in 2025, with a compound annual growth rate of 21.5%. By region, North America accounts for the largest share of the current NLP market, but the Asia Pacific region is the market with the most potential in the NLP industry and will become the region with the highest growth rate in the next few years.

NLP technologies are being used in more and more smart products and applications. Typical applications such as dialogue-based smart assistants including Apple Siri, Google Assistant, Amazon Alexa, Baidu DuerOS, Xiaomi voice assistant, and many other systems, which with the development of smart speakers, have penetrated into everyone's life. According to the report of the authoritative research organization Strategy Analytics [16], global smart speaker sales was 147 million units in 2019, reaching a record high, with a year-on-year increase of 70%. Although the covid-19 epidemic in early 2020 has had a great impact on the entire smart speaker market, and offline sales channels almost stagnated in February, global smart speaker shipments in the first quarter of 2020 still reached 28.2 million units, an increase of 8.2% year-on-year. Amazon has always occupied the first place in global sales, followed by Google, Baidu, Alibaba, and Xiaomi.

In terms of market share, tech giants dominate the market, but there are still opportunities for small and medium-sized companies in subdivisions. At present, Google, Amazon, Apple, Facebook, Microsoft, Baidu, Alibaba, Tencent, and other tech titans occupy an absolute dominant position in the NLP market. They continue to expand their global influence, provide innovative solutions, and increase market share and profitability through mergers and acquisitions. However, in the technological subdivision of NLP, there are some excellent small and medium-sized enterprises, like Narrative Science, Yseop, and others. As many countries have introduced policies to support investment in startups, industrial innovation has also begun to accelerate. As of 2017, the number of cognitive and smart startups in the U.S. was nearly 250, distributed in various vertical fields, such as finance, healthcare, and e-commerce. At the same time, many traditional companies have acquired NLP startups. For example, McDonald's has acquired three language-related AI companies since 2018 and set up an AI laboratory in Silicon Valley.

1.3.2   Diversified NLP Applications

With the constant expansion of the NLP market, the application forms are also increasing. NLP technologies have been extensively used in the fields of search, finance, law, e-commerce, healthcare, and others.

NLP technologies are widely applied in the Internet field. By integrating a large number of open source knowledge bases and user data, Google has developed a search function based on knowledge graphs to make search results more accurate, intuitive, and personalized. By mining its global social network data, Facebook built a social graph named Open Graph, based on the interpersonal social relationships. In early 2019, Facebook added new features to Stories, the product based on social graphs, which facilitates people to share their interesting events and activities through Stories and coordinates people's meeting with friends. Twitter built interest relationships between people and things through interest graphs. Netflix constructed a knowledge graph based on the registration information and viewing behavior data of its subscribers, and launched new online dramas based on the analysis results of users' preferences. In China, relying on its strong accumulation in search, Baidu has taken the lead in the research and application of Chinese knowledge graphs, and has made constant progress. Sogou's Knowledge Cube and Alibaba's Shenma Search also use general knowledge graphs in their search products to meet the knowledge acquisition needs of users. In addition, Sina Weibo has constructed a social graph, and Alibaba optimizes the user's shopping experience based on the product Knowledge Graph.

Machine translation is becoming more mature, and multiple technologies are combined to enhance user experience. MT quality continues to improve and has provided people with convenient services in tourism, daily conversation, news, and other fields. Application forms have been constantly expanded. In addition to text translation, there is a strong demand for translation of various types of documents. It is necessary to keep corresponding format information during translation, like fonts, colors, tables, formulas, graphics, and others, which can greatly improve the efficiency when translating manuals, contracts, reports, and other documents. With the fast development of diverse mobile devices and network technologies, translation needs and scenarios have become more diversified. For example, photo translation and augmented reality translation combined with computer vision technology are widely used in menus, street signs, animation, and other scenarios to improve user experience. Voice translation combined with speech technology makes input more convenient and efficient and is broadly used in scenarios such as overseas travel, daily conversation, and conference presentation.

Intelligent customer service based on human-machine dialogue has become a powerful guarantee for reducing costs and increasing efficiency in the service industry. At present, many customer services in financial, marketing, and other service industries have been completed by robots. To mine, sort, index, and analyze industry know-how based on knowledge graph technology, People can build a knowledge base in the corresponding field, and provide flexible support for various service scenarios in a modular fashion. For instance, Indian HDFC Bank cooperated with Senseforth to launch an electronic virtual assistant, EVA, based on NLP and speech technologies, which has processed 2.7 million queries within 6 months. In China, Alibaba Xiaomi is a dedicated AI customer service robot for Taobao and Tmall users. During the Double11 Shopping Festival in 2019, it undertook 97% of the online customer service on Taobao and Tmall platforms and completed 300 million consultations, equivalent to 85,000 customer service staff members.

Through NLP technologies, complex knowledge management systems have been built in a variety of fields. In fields of corporate office, Microsoft introduced the knowledge graph function Project Cortex for Microsoft 365 in 2019, which aims to use the knowledge network built by AI technologies to reason about internal and external data in the organization, to automatically sort out the data into shared topics according to the relevance of the projects or customers, and to send the related knowledge to relevant internal personnel. In addition, Project Cortex can transform the information of the organization into an interactive knowledge base, which is updated continuously and iteratively, and a more complex content model would be iterated out by analyzing relevant documents and users' feedback. Project Cortex focuses on "collecting and managing knowledge", "recognizing, understanding, and summarizing knowledge", "applying acquired knowledge" and "transforming knowledge into a process of accelerating learning and sharing." Microsoft officially launched the English version in the first half of 2020 and gradually expanded to other language versions. Baidu has launched an AI office platform "InfoFlow" in 2020, which integrates corporate communication, collaborative office, and knowledge management, and is committed to making intelligent office work smooth so that the information and knowledge in the company can greatly improve work efficiency and inspire innovations.

In the financial field, NLP technologies automatically extract valuable information from semi-structured data such as prospectus, financial reports, brokerage research and analysis reports, consulting analysis reports, investment reports and financial news, to build a knowledge graph to provide various analytical data for investment. In the event of macroeconomic or corporate emergencies, it can make a deeper analysis and more accurate investment decision in time, and can also carry out risk analysis and fraud identification to control financial risks. Top international investment banks such as Goldman Sachs, JP Morgan, and Citibank have carried out relevant explorations and applications in this field. Kensho Technologies, based on the Warren Q&A engine, established the correlation between events and assets by monitoring various information sources such as financial report releases, global data environment, economic reports, company product releases, and drug approvals from the U.S. FDA (Food and Drug Administration) to predict asset price trends for investment companies.

In the medical and health field, NLP technology has broader application prospects. Modern medical materials including papers and data are voluminous, and new medical methods are constantly evolving. No doctor or expert can understand and master all the medical knowledge. However, NLP technology can help doctors and experts quickly and accurately find the latest research progress of a great number of difficult diseases so that patients can enjoy the fruits of medical technology progress more quickly. Based on the NLP technology and medical knowledge graphs, it can realize the auxiliary input of medical records, the retrieval and analysis of medical data, intelligent triage, clinical auxiliary diagnosis, intelligent inquiry, virus analysis, new drug development, and more.

In the legal field, NLP technologies can be explored to understand court cases, documents, files, news, and more, which plays an important role in ensuring the uniformity of judicial criteria and judgment standards. It can also assist in case searching, legal document generation, legal material translation, and others.

In addition, NLP technology has been widely applied in smart cities, smart education, smart homes, smart media, and other fields. A large amount of data generated by various applications in turn helps to optimize models and improve application effects. NLP technologies will be more deeply integrated with the real economy, facing more complex scenarios, dealing with more complicated issues, accelerating the intelligent upgrading of traditional industries, and providing momentum for the constant creation of new applications, new models, and new businesses.

1.3.3 Open-Source Platform and Ecosystem Accelerating Industrial Intelligent Transformation

1. Open source lowers the barriers to R&D and application.

As NLP technology becomes more mature, open source for developers and enterprises has greatly lowered the barriers to R&D and application, and enlarged the production capacity of NLP technology.

Research and academic institutions have always had a tradition of open source. Among the most famous ones include the NLP toolkit CoreNLP from Stanford University, the language technology platform LTP from Harbin Institute of Technology, and FNLP from Fudan University. These toolkits provide a set of essential NLP algorithms and models, such as POS tagging, NER, syntactic parsing, semantic role labelling, language model, anaphora resolution, sentiment analysis, and others. In addition, most mainstream programming languages are also integrated with NLP libraries. For example, the most popular Python NLP packages are NLTK, a Natural Language Toolkit widely used for teaching and research, developed by University of Pennsylvania, and SpaCy, which is designed for industrial products. And the most common Java NLP library is Apache OpenNLP.

Tech giants have also made efforts to build algorithm and model tool libraries, package them, and make them available to developers on platform. With the prevalence of deep learning, mainstream deep learning frameworks have integrated NLP libraries and pre-trained models. For example, Facebook has developed an NLP modeling framework PyText, which is used to achieve rapid development, deployment, and application of NLP models in PyTorch. Google's TensorFlow integrates its powerful language model Transformer and pre-trained model BERT, and open-sources the text processing library TF.Text. Many third-party organizations and developers in China and abroad have developed and open-sourced a large number of NLP models and toolkits based on PyTorch and TensorFlow. For example, AI2 built the NLP platform AllenNLP based on PyTorch. The NLP toolkit and Transformer series models created by Chatbot developer Hugging Face support both PyTorch and TensorFlow. In China, Baidu opened up industrial-grade Chinese NLP tools and model libraries within PaddleNLP in 2019. PaddleNLP is based on the self-developed deep learning platform PaddlePaddle. It provides 35 basic NLP algorithms and models such as lexical analysis, semantic representation, and text classification and supports eight types of NLP tasks including reading comprehension, dialogue system, among others. By September 2020, there are more than 2.3 million developers active on PaddlePaddle platform, including more than 90,000 enterprises to build 300,000 AI models.

2. Cloud service speeds up industrialization of NLP technologies.

AI applications driven by deep learning technology often require huge computing power, and AI open platform based on cloud services can provide greater production capacity. Global cloud services and AI giants, like Amazon, Microsoft, Google, Alibaba, Baidu, Tencent, and others have taken full advantage of their own strengths and committed to creating AI cloud platforms that cover speech, computer vision, and NLP technologies.

Amazon Web Services (AWS) is the world's largest public cloud service, and AI is the key feature of its layout. There are two mature products for NLP. One is Amazon Comprehend focusing on natural language understanding, that can help customers discover opinions and relationships in text through machine learning. The other is Amazon Lex, which can help customers build dialogue services based on voice and text.

Google Cloud Services provides specialized AI and machine learning products. The basic AI components for NLP include AutoML Natural Language, which allows users to build their own models, and Natural Language API, based on pre-trained language models, to complete NLP tasks like syntax parsing, entity recognition, sentiment analysis, and content classification. It also provides components such as multi-language translation, speech-to-text conversion, dialogue management, and others.

Microsoft's Azure AI cloud platform integrates knowledge mining, machine learning, and AI applications and services. Knowledge mining makes use of OCR, ASR and NLP technologies such as NER, key phrase extraction, language detection, and sentiment analysis to extract latent knowledge from a large number of different types of data. The machine learning platform assists developers to fast generate, build, and deploy their own AI models. Finally, Azure Cognitive Services provide corresponding language applications and services based on the trained models, such as speech-to-text conversion, intent recognition, machine translation, and dialogue robots, among others.

Baidu's AI platform on Baidu Cloud opens more than 270 AI capabilities by September 2020. Its NLP section includes not only basic technologies such as entity annotation, syntactic parsing, and semantic representation, but also application platforms such as machine translation, language generation, and language understanding and interaction. Baidu's cloud services also provide computing resources, allowing developers to quickly implement system development based on leading technologies and platforms. By September 2020, the total number of developers exceeds 2.3 million.

Open-source platforms and ecosystems support developers to accelerate technological innovation and greatly improve the R&D and production efficiency of industrial applications. It is of great significance to improve social productivity and accelerate the intelligent transformation and upgrading of traditional industries.

Chapter 2
Development Status in China

In the process of technological revolution and industrial transformation driven by the new generation of artificial intelligence, China highly values and promotes the healthy development of AI. In recent years, NLP, as one of the core fields of AI research, has rapidly developed in all respects. For example, it maintains the leading position in fields of knowledge graph construction and application, semantic analysis, machine translation, and others, and meanwhile, it continues to narrow the gap with the world's leading level in fundamental theories and underlying technologies. In terms of technology application and industry promotion, China is in the first echelon of the world. Innovative technologies drive industrial development, and applications and products such as intelligent search, machine translation, and smart speakers have penetrated into people's daily life, which not only changes the way people obtain information, knowledge, and service, but also further promotes the intelligent development of social economy.

2.1   Top Planning and Overall Layout to Create Strategic Environment for Innovative Development

The development of NLP and knowledge graphs has great significance for advancing the transition of AI from perceptual intelligence to cognitive intelligence, accelerating the industrial application of AI, and making an important impact on economic and social development.

On July 8, 2017, Chinese State Council formally issued the *New Generation Artificial Intelligence Development Plan*, proposing to "construct an open and cooperative AI technology innovation system. In view of the weak foundation in original theories and the lack of major products and systems, we shall establish fundamental theories and a key general technology system for a new generation of AI, construct major scientific and technological innovation base, strengthen the AI

Chinese Academy of Engineering, *The Development of Natural Language Processing*, https://doi.org/10.1007/978-981-16-1986-1_2

high-end talent, promote innovation and cooperative interactions and form contin-uous innovation ability of AI [17]". Among the eight key generic AI technologies mentioned, there are four tasks involving NLP, covering techniques of knowledge acquisition, knowledge reasoning, language analysis, semantic understanding, human-machine conversation, and others. The Plan provides strong support for grasping the major strategic opportunities for AI development and building an innovative environment for science and technology.

In December 2017, the Ministry of Industry and Information Technology formu-lated the "Three-Year Action Plan for Promoting Development of a New Generation Artificial Intelligence Industry (2018–2020)," implementing the "New Generation Artificial Intelligence Development Plan" to promote the development of the AI industry. Among them, machine translation is listed as one of the important fields: "Promote the application of high-precision intelligent translation systems, and use machine learning techniques to enhance the accuracy and practicability for typical scenarios such as multilingual translation and simultaneous interpretation."

In March 2020, the Standing Committee of the Political Bureau of the CPC Central Committee held a meeting focusing on accelerating the construction of new infrastructure such as 5G networks, data centers, and AI, which laid a firm founda-tion for the development of AI, and also provided a strong guarantee for NLP to be fully implemented in practical application scenarios.

2.2   Overall Equivalent to the World Advanced Level

2.2.1   The State of the Overall Development

In the first two stages of NLP technology, namely the rationalism stage based on rules and symbolic methods and the empiricism stage based on statistical machine learning, the overall level of technological development in China is far behind advanced foreign countries. In recent years, NLP technology has shifted to deep learning methods. Although we are still facing a situation of weak theoretical foundation, China has been catching up rapidly and has reached the world's top level in some core technologies. The number of academic papers, patents, et al. is growing rapidly. Not only have we seen more scholars from China at international academic conferences, but also many top international conferences such as the ACL have been held in China, increasing the voice of Chinese scholars in the field of NLP. Moreover, relying on a good technological and industrial ecology, China has certain leading advantages in terms of applications.

ACL is the top international academic organization in the field of NLP. It is also one of the most influential and active international academic organizations in the world, representing the highest level of computational linguistics. In 2020, ACL received paper submissions from 57 countries. Among them, the United States and China led in the number of submissions, accounting for 64% of the total. China ranked first with 1084 and the U.S. is second with 1039. The United Kingdom and

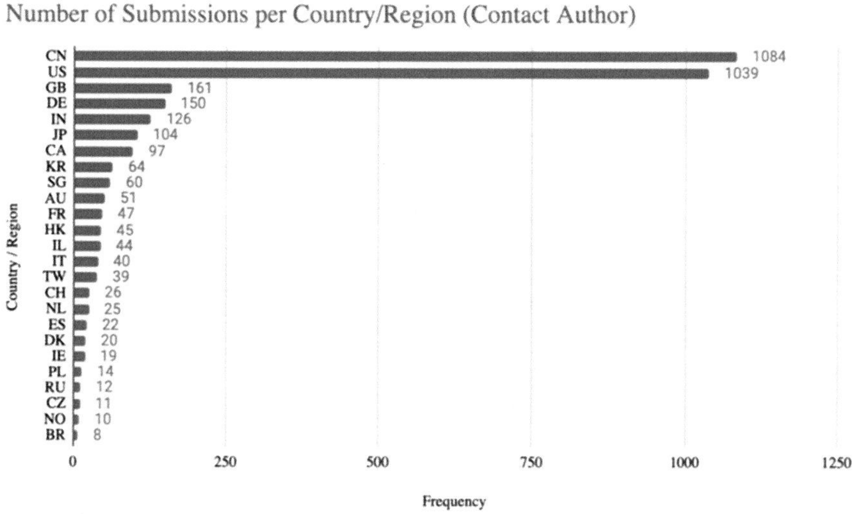

Number of Submissions per Country/Region (Contact Author)

Fig. 2.1 Number of Submissions per Country/Region of ACL 2020 (Top 25 countries/regions)

Germany ranked third and fourth with 161 and 150, respectively. From the perspective of paper awards, at the ACL 2019, Chinese research teams won the best long paper and two outstanding paper awards; and in 2020, two Chinese students were awarded the best long paper and the best demo paper, that fully demonstrates the academic strength and influence of Chinese scholars (Fig. 2.1).

Although Chinese paper submissions are the most, the paper acceptance rate is not high. In ACL 2020, it was less than 19%, much lower than Israel (40.9%), the UK (31.1%), the US (29.4%), and Germany (29.3%), indicating that China's overall scientific research level still has much room for improvement.

In the knowledge graph field, Fig. 2.2 shows the comparison of the number of academic papers on knowledge graphs published by Chinese and foreign research institutions at the top NLP conferences in the past 3 years (2017–2019). It is clear that foreign research institutions still have certain advantages in terms of comprehensiveness and advancement of technology. In the aspect of knowledge acquisition, Chinese research institutions focus on entity recognition and relation extraction, while foreign research institutions pay more attention to the whole process of knowledge graph construction and quality control. In the aspect of knowledge application, search and Q&A are the most studied application scenarios worldwide. In recent years, application exploration in medical care, finance, manufacturing, education, and other fields has gradually increased. In addition, with the great success of unsupervised pre-training method in the field of NLP, how to use knowledge to guide unsupervised pre-training has rapidly become the focus of academia and industry.

Regarding patents, *"2019 Analysis Report of China's Artificial Intelligence Patents"* released by National Industrial Information Security Development

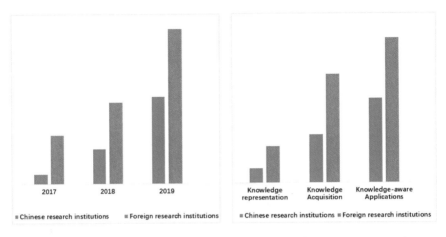

Fig. 2.2 Comparison in knowledge graphs between Chinese and foreign research institutions

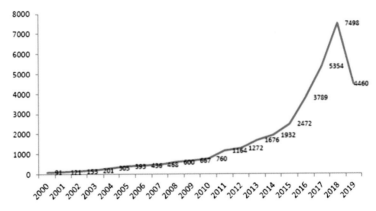

Fig. 2.3 Trend of annual filings of NLP patents in China (due to the publication delay, patent data disclosure in 2019 is incomplete)

Research Center shows the changes in the number of patent applications of NLP technologies in China over the years. Under the circumstance that AI technologies and applications continue to attract attention, the number of NLP technology patents filed is going higher and higher. In 2000, a total of 91 patents related to NLP were filed nationwide, and by 2018, a total of 7498 patents were filed, accounting for an 80-times increase (Fig. 2.3).

According to the number of applicants, Baidu ranked first with 938. The leading advantage is so obvious that reflects Baidu's technical superiority in the field of NLP. There are three universities among the top ten: Beihang University the sixth, Zhejiang University the seventh, and Tsinghua University the tenth. There is little difference in the number of applicants between them, indicating that universities and research institutes also have certain advantages in this field (Fig. 2.4).

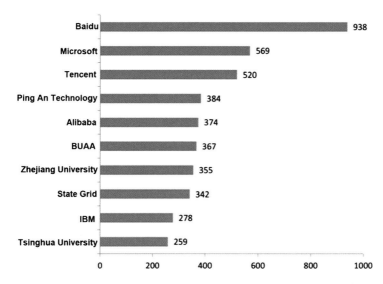

Fig. 2.4 Top ten companies/universities/institutions in patent filings

In addition, compared with other countries, China has obvious advantages in the number of patent filings in the field of NLP. In 2019, Hurun Report and WTOIP, an intellectual property and sci-tech innovation platform, jointly released *2019 White Paper on Intellectual Property Development in China's Artificial Intelligence Industry*. According to the White Paper, for the first half of 2019, the number of global NLP-related patent filings exceeded 113,000, showing a big increase overall. China, the U.S., Japan, and South Korea have been the most active in patent filings in this field, especially China, who has maintained the leading position since it surpassed the U.S., Japan, and South Korea for the first time in 2009.

In recent years, with the fast development of AI in China, many universities, institutes, and companies have carried out systematic and in-depth research and applications of NLP and knowledge graph technology. In this process, China's achievements have gradually been recognized by the international academic community. At the same time, a large number of experts and scholars have gained global reputation, creating more influence in the international arena. In 2013, Dr. Haifeng Wang was elected as the president of ACL, becoming the first president from China in ACL's history. In 2015, the ACL annual conference was held in mainland China (Beijing) for the first time. Professor Sheng Li was honored the ACL Lifetime Achievement Award for his outstanding contributions in machine translation and other fields. He is the first Chinese scholar in the world to receive this honor. In July 2018, The Asia-Pacific Chapter of Association for Computational Linguistics (AACL) was launched, with Dr. Haifeng Wang as the founding chair. This indicates that the academic influence of Asia-Pacific region is getting stronger and stronger.

2.2.2 Development Status of Key Technologies

The goal of NLP is to enable machines to use knowledge, understand language, and think like human beings. The following introduces key technologies and application progress in the field of NLP in China.

To some extent, knowledge may be regarded as the ladder for AI to get progress, and the research on knowledge engineering runs through the entire history of AI. In recent years, knowledge graph technology has developed rapidly in China. Baidu, Alibaba, JD.com, Sogou, and other enterprises have successively constructed large-scale application-oriented knowledge graphs, among which the super large-scale knowledge graph constructed by Baidu consists of more than five billion entities and more than 550 billion facts. Large-scale knowledge graph is not only the cornerstone of natural language semantic understanding, but also laying foundations for cross-modal deep semantic understanding.

Natural language understanding is one of the key technologies in the field of NLP. In recent years, "pre-training" has become a general paradigm since J. Devlin, Chang, et al. proposed BERT. On this basis, Tsinghua University and Baidu respectively proposed the idea of introducing knowledge to help improve the learning ability of neural network models, which has raised the performance of semantic understanding to a new level and refreshed the effects of a wide range of NLP tasks. Baidu's ERNIE [18] broke the 90-point mark for the first time in the GLUE evaluation, causing a sensation in the international arena. It was appraised by the authoritative technology magazine *MIT Technology Review* as "Baidu has a new trick for teaching AI the meaning of language."

Since the beginning of twenty-first century, the research and development of language generation in China has gradually reached the international top range and even has a certain leading advantage in some specific fields. In respect of Chinese language generation, it has absolute technical and resource advantages. It is worth noting that the technology of Chinese poetry generation continues to present in international academic conferences, which not only features distinctive technologies, but also plays a potential role in cultural communication to a certain extent.

Machine translation is a classical task in the NLP field. China's MT technology is at the forefront of the world. In terms of translation quality, Baidu, Alibaba, Tencent, Sogou, and iFLYTEK have won championships on multiple tracks in the international authoritative machine translation evaluation WMT (Workshop on Machine Translation) in recent years. In particular, in May 2015, Baidu officially launched the world's first Internet neural network translation system to provide online service, while Google did not launch a similar neural network translation system until September 2016, more than a year later. As to simultaneous interpretation, many Chinese companies have carried out research in this field and have made great progress. In 2018, *MIT Technology Review* listed voice translation as the world's top ten breakthrough technologies, and Baidu and Google were listed as key players.

Search engine is one of the most important applications of NLP technology. With the rapid development of informationization and digitization, and complex user demands, the keyword queries and simple webpage results are far from satisfying. For example, the query input by users is no longer a keyword, but a natural language question; or users' input is no longer limited to text, but also includes voice, images, and more. Users expect more accurate results, which can be directly displayed on small screens of mobile phones, or even on smart speakers. The results include not only text, but also multi-modal resources such as tables, images, voices, and videos. These new features have put forward higher requirements for cross-modal deep semantic understanding, knowledge reasoning, and other technologies. Baidu and Google, relying on their long-term advantages on technology, industrial practice and talent, lead the Chinese and English search, respectively.

2.3 Strong Market Demands Industry Entities to Expand

With the increasing number of AI applications and the continuous penetration of AI-powered products in daily life, companies from all over the world have increased their R&D investment in AI technologies. According to *2020 China AI Basic Data Service Industry Development Report* released by iResearch, the R&D expense in 2019 of Chinese tech companies is about 400.5 billion yuan, of which AI related R&D expense most from internet tech companies, exceeds 37 billion yuan, accounting for 9.3%. The R&D expense in NLP accounts for 7.1%, which is about 2.6 billion yuan. Computer vision accounted for 22.5%, and speech recognition/synthesis accounted for 2.3%. In addition to internet tech giants, there are nearly 100 NLP startups (Fig. 2.5).

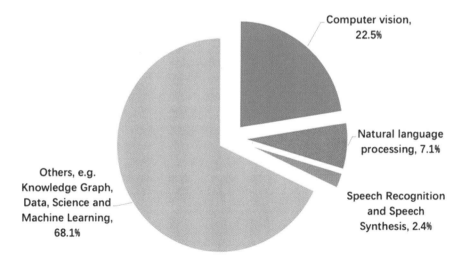

Source : iresearch，2020 China AI Basic Data Service Industry Development Report

Fig. 2.5 R&D expense in AI main areas by Chinese high-tech companies in 2019

Table 2.1 2019 Smart Speaker Analysis released by Canalys (sell-in shipments)

Vendor	2019 Shipments (million)	2019 Market share	2018 Shipments (million)	2018 Market share	Annual growth
Amazon	37.3	29.90%	24.2	31.10%	+54%
Google	23.8	19.10%	23.4	30.00%	+2%
Baidu	17.3	13.90%	3.6	4.60%	+384%
Alibaba	16.8	13.50%	8.9	11.40%	+89%
Xiaomi	14.1	11.30%	7.1	9.10%	+97%
Others	15.4	12.30%	10.8	13.80%	+43%
Total	124.6	100.00%	78	100.00%	+60%

The big investment from enterprises has effectively boosted the applications and the industrial landing of NLP technologies. Whether in a mature or a new scenario, it is full of vitality due to the introduction of new technologies.

In mature scenarios, on one hand, new technologies continue to improve the effect and quality to meet the demands; on the other hand, they continue to expand the scope of applications to promote the intelligent development of social economy. Take machine translation as an example: through the internet, people can obtain information from all over the world in real time and make friends with people from any other countries. It becomes reality that "a talented person will know the world without going out." However, according to incomplete statistics, 80% of the web pages on the internet are non-Chinese. The language gap is a common problem faced by everyone. Besides, from 1995 to 2019, the number of outbound tourists from China increased from five million to 155 million [19]. Tourist destinations cover most countries and regions in the world, and the demand for multi-lingual and multi-scenario translation has risen sharply.

In new scenarios, NLP technology plays an irreplaceable role in products and scenarios such as smart homes, information recommendation, video recommendation, intelligent customer service, intelligent maps and navigation, local life services, and others, affecting the daily lives of hundreds of millions people. In the intelligent age, with the continuous expansion of user demands and progress of NLP technologies, there is a huge potential market. Take smart speakers equipped with NLP and other technologies as an example: according to the 2019 smart speaker shipment report released by the international authoritative research organization Canalys in February 2020, China's smart speaker shipments in 2019 doubled to 52 million units compared with shipments in 2018. Particularly, Baidu's smart speaker shipments achieved an amazing growth of 384%, with the sales volume of 3.6 million units in 2018, and 17.3 million units in 2019. The total sales growth of Baidu, Alibaba, and Xiaomi in China accounted for 64% of global growth (Table 2.1) [20].

In addition to greatly satisfying people's daily needs, new technologies have also played an important role in industry applications. NLP technologies have become more widely used in finance, healthcare, e-commerce, media, and other fields.

In the finance field, AlphaInsight Technology developed an IPO audit system for the investment banking department of financial institutions, providing functions such as typo identification, third-party comparison, and document consistency detection.

In the e-commerce field, Alibaba and Leyan Technology have cooperated to launch Taobao smart customer service, which gives priority to robots to answer some questions, and return to human service when they encounter unanswered questions. The intelligent customer service robot JIMI launched by JD.com judges customers' emotions based on the sentiment analysis of users, so as to give smarter and warmer responses.

In the field of media, Baidu launched Intelligent Writing Platform, including auto writing and writing assistant, to promote news timing and efficiency and eventually to free more people to create better news.

In the medical field, the clinical decision support system (CDSS) provided by Baidu can diagnose disease based on patients' symptoms, or infer future symptoms based on specific diseases. Yitu Technology and Tencent Ruizhi cooperated with Guangzhou Women and Children's Medical Center to launch a medical consultation mini program called "inquire bear," which can identify 518 kinds of diseases related to women and children, covering more than 95% of common diseases in the field. The accuracy rate for doctor recommendation is as high as 97.3%.

The covid-19 epidemic in early 2020 has severely affected people's work and life. Under the new situation, a number of products and applications based on NLP technologies, such as AI medical consultation and intelligent call centers, have emerged rapidly to provide people with smarter and more humanized services.

Chapter 3
Trends and Highlights in China

3.1 Knowledge Graph

Great progress has been witnessed in KG technology and applications. KG is now one of the most representative technologies of knowledge engineering in the era of big data and has been put into large-scale implementation in Search, Question Answering, and other simple scenarios. China's strong concern and continued commitment to innovation in KG technology and applications in the past few years have resulted in a lot of progress and breakthroughs. Key issues and highlights will be elaborated on from both a technology and application perspective.

3.1.1 Development and Hot Topics of KG

With the vigorous development of artificial intelligence, China has seen unprecedented progress in KG in recent years. Current trends and highlights are outlined below.

1. The automatic construction of large-scale KG has made breakthrough, and KG begins to be widely used in industrial applications.

AI technology breakthroughs and massive data have laid the foundation for the automatic construction of knowledge graphs. However, the core technology of large-scale knowledge graph is still possessed by a few technology giants with sufficient data, computing power and algorithm resources, such as Google and Baidu. Baidu took the lead in exploring the automatic construction of knowledge graphs among tech companies in China, and developed a complete automatic knowledge mining system for massive, multi-source and multi-form data [21], as shown in Fig. 3.1. This knowledge mining system uses multi-dimensional data analysis and language understanding technology to break through the technical

Chinese Academy of Engineering, *The Development of Natural Language Processing*, https://doi.org/10.1007/978-981-16-1986-1_3

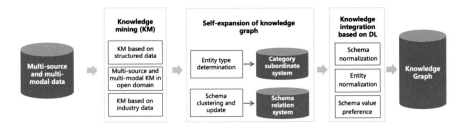

Fig. 3.1 Technical Framework for Automatic Construction of Ultra-large-scale KG

bottleneck of learning large-scale structured knowledge from massive unstructured data. At the same time, the system proposes the entity normalization technology based on semantic space transformation to realize the normalization of multi-source open domain large-scale entities. The integration of normalization solves the problems of diverse knowledge representation and difficulty in relational integration. In addition, the combination between automatic learning of the knowledge and the open knowledge mining completes the transition of the knowledge system from manual editing to automatic construction, realizing the automatic knowledge expansion and active knowledge collection. Based on this system, Baidu constructed an ultra-large-scale multi-source knowledge graph with more than 5 billion entities and 550 billion facts, establishing a whole process mechanism from knowledge graph construction to application. In addition, Xiaomi also cooperated with Tsinghua University, Zhejiang University, etc. to release the OpenBase project, which is dedicated to knowledge extraction, mining, and integration, and realizes knowledge update and crowdsourcing to serve the Chinese knowledge graph community.

2. Knowledge representation, mining, and application based on deep learning become trends.

Deep learning is one of the hottest foundational technologies today and has gained significant results in many scenarios. It is penetrating the knowledge graph life cycle from knowledge representation to knowledge mining and to knowledge-aware application. For knowledge representation, the early exploration is that Richard Socher et al. proposed Neural Tensor Network [22] to learn the representation of knowledge graph in 2013. Chinese scholars and research institutes have also focused on using deep neural networks and graph neural networks to learn knowledge graph representations. University of Science and Technology of China proposed Neural Association Model (NAM), which uses multi-layer perceptron to calculate the correlation coefficient of triple-type knowledge items to measure its authenticity. Tsinghua University proposed Path-based Translating Embedding (PTransE), which uses RNN to model the association path between entities and provide additional evidence for determining the relationship between entities. Tsinghua also released Text-Enhanced Knowledge Embedding (TEKE), which uses the text information of the co-realistic entity to

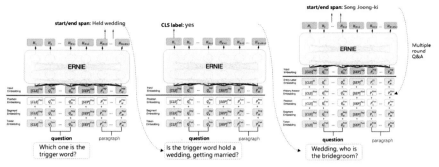

Paragraph: on October 31, 2017, Song Joong-ki and Song Hye-kyo held their wedding in Seoul

Fig. 3.2   Event extraction model based on deep learning

enhance the representation of neighbor entities. These knowledge representation learning methods can effectively express discrete symbolic knowledge graphs in continuous vectorized format, so that prior knowledge in KGs can be used more conveniently and effectively by downstream tasks.

For knowledge mining, many deep learning models have been able to effectively complete end-to-end named entity recognition, relation extraction, knowledge graph completion, and knowledge fusion to build or scale up knowledge graphs. The Chinese Academy of Sciences has proposed some relation extraction systems based on CNN and RNN. The core idea is to use CNN and RNN to extract contextual features between entities to determine their semantic relation. Baidu uses deep learning models for the integration and completion of large-scale knowledge graphs, as well as more complex event knowledge extraction and domain knowledge extraction [23]. For example, as shown in Fig. 3.2, Baidu transforms the task of event extraction into multiple rounds of Q&A, and uses multiple rounds of reading comprehension technology based on deep learning to sequentially realize event trigger word recognition, event type determination, and event argument extraction.

In terms of knowledge application, more deep learning models provide new solutions for many downstream tasks, including KG-based question answering, recommendations, etc.

3. Using knowledge-enhanced machine learning models to solve problems is now mainstream.

Current machine learning is data-driven, learning statistical clues from vast amounts of data to deal with practical tasks. However, many tasks, where prior knowledge is indispensable, are beyond the ability of data-driven machine learning models. Integrating symbolic knowledge with statistical machine learning models is becoming a main approach to solve the problem. The University of Science and Technology of China designed a linguistic knowledge enhanced co-attention mechanism to improve the natural language inference of Bidirectional Long

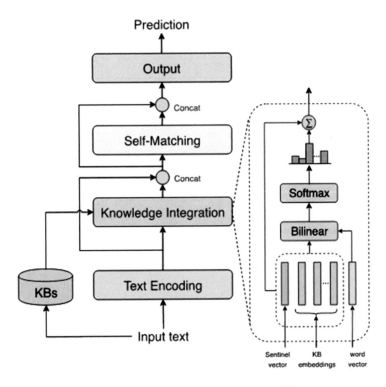

Fig. 3.3 Deep neural network model integrated with symbolic knowledge

Short-Term Memory [24].The KT-NET, jointly developed by Baidu and Peking University, uses linguistic knowledge and fact-based knowledge simultaneously to improve the effect of deep neural networks on machine reading comprehension tasks [25]. KT-NET structure is shown in Fig. 3.3: text coding layer represents a given question chapter; the knowledge integration layer automatically filters and integrates knowledge highly related to the question text from the knowledge graph through the attention mechanism; self-matching layer uses double-layer self-attention matching to model multiple interaction, realizing deep fusion, between text and knowledge; the output layer predicts the knowledge-oriented answer boundary based on the integration representation. The knowledge-enhanced models are able to increase the use of prior knowledge and improve their results' consistency with prior knowledge on one hand, lower the dependency on large sample sizes, and raise the efficiency of learning on the other. This approach seems to have more positive benefits to vertical industries with sparse data and abundant expert knowledge.

4. KG and NLP are embarking on a path of synergy.

KG is an interdisciplinary combination of knowledge engineering, machine learning, NLP, and other technologies. Rapid progress in NLP over the past few years has given KG more possibilities. Driven by deep learning and big data, language intelligence has moved forward in great leaps since 2018. The new paradigm of unsupervised pre-training followed by supervised fine-tuning has had a huge success on a variety of language cognition tasks. Pre-training language models can fully capture syntactic and semantic information in natural language data, while fine-tuning further adapts the general-purpose models to specific tasks. For one thing, how to use knowledge to guide pre-training or fine-tuning has become a focus in both academia and industry. For another, the pre-training plus fine-tuning paradigm is very friendly to data-sparse vertical industries and is expected to give full play of its strength in industry knowledge acquisition.

3.1.2 Hot Industrial Applications

Besides general-purpose use, KG has a broad range of applications in healthcare, finance, education, law, security, government, and other industries. Now in China, KG applications, no matter for general-purpose or for industrial use, are booming.

1. General-purpose Applications

General-purpose applications include search engines, question answering and rec-
    ommendation systems, and others. Currently the core technology of general-
    purpose KG is held by a few internet giants with adequate data, computing, and
    algorithm resources, such as search engine companies like Baidu and Google.
    Baidu introduced KG technology in search products like Zhixin in as early as
    2011, aggregating information from multiple dimensions for users. In 2014 Baidu
    officially released a KG-based precise answering product, improving search
    experience by presenting answers to objective queries. Furthermore, search
    engines can use KG to give quality recommendations and tell users why such
    recommendations are given. Figure 3.4 displays some KG-based products in
    Baidu Search. Other search engines such as Sogou, Shenma, and Bing Search
    also have similar products.

2. Industrial Applications

As the national strategy of artificial intelligence is moving forward across industries,
    we start to see a shift in KG applications, from general-purpose to more industry-
    specific. Information-oriented industries such as healthcare, finance, law, and
    education are at the forefront of KG application. Leading enterprises in these
    industries all have released their KG-based products.
Healthcare Industry: According to the 2019 Statistical Report on the Development of
    China's Medical and Health Services, there are now 3.86 million registered
    medical practitioners in China. The total number of medical visits across the
    country reached 8.72 billion in 2019, indicating an extreme supply and demand
    imbalance between doctors and patients. This imbalance has been particularly

Fig. 3.4 KG-based Products in Baidu Search

Table 3.1 Medical KGs' application potential and representative products

Intelligent medical products	KGs' application potential	Representative products
AI-assisted diagnosis	Clinical decision support, prescription automatic screening, clinical data insights, medical record quality control, etc.	Baidu doctor, PingAn healthcare, Ali health
Intelligent patient service	Health knowledge push, health assessment, intelligent triage, etc.	Baidu doctor, WeDoctor, Tencent AIMIS
Medical research	Disease risk prediction, medicine research, drug discovery, medical evidence mining, etc.	Huawei EIHealth, StoneWise, Atman

prominent during the 2020 COVID-19 epidemic. Knowledge systems and applications supported by medical knowledge graphs can liberate doctors from heavy and repetitive work and improve the efficiency and quality of medical services. Main applications of knowledge graphs in the medical industry include AI-assisted diagnosis, intelligent patient services, medical research, and more.

Table 3.2   Financial KGs' application potential and product overview

Intelligent financial products	KGs' application potential
Intelligent risk management	Data consistency check for fraud detection throughout the whole process of lending, investment, and insurance
Intelligent investment research	Information extraction and heterogeneous data linking based on enterprises' announcements, annual reports, news articles and other text, intelligent QA, and intelligent reasoning for investment analysis and decision making
Robo-advisor	Structuralizing or linking data of stocks, funds, bonds, transactions, etc. for automated or semi-automated asset allocation
Intelligent marketing	Linking various data sources for profiling user community and planning marketing strategies
Intelligent customer service	Intelligent QA to raise the ratio of auto-response and users' satisfaction

Table 3.1 lists the application potential and key products of medical knowledge graphs.

Financial Industry: The financial industry has seen very active applications of AI. In the New Generation Artificial Intelligence Development Plan issued by the State Council, smart finance is listed as a key area of the development of high-end smart economy. According to International Data Corporation (IDC), 80% of worldwide financial data is unstructured, fragmented, and of variable quality. Financial knowledge graphs can solve the problem and promote the transformation and upgrade of traditional financial business, lower cost, and improve efficiency. They are mainly used in intelligent risk management, intelligent investment research, robot-advisor, intelligent marketing, intelligent customer service, and more, as shown in Table 3.2.

Law Industry: Currently AI technologies are driving a deep revolution in the law industry. The construction of smart courts and intelligent procurator work have equal importance as judicial system reforms [26]. It badly needs legal knowledge graphs for similar case recommendation, intelligent sentencing, juridical document generation, and legal document error correction.

Education Industry: The artificial intelligent education market has huge potential. Internet giants such as Baidu, Tencent, and Alibaba, and leading education enterprises such as New Oriental, Genshuixue, and Haoweilai all have plans in AI and education. Educational knowledge graphs are in great demand for intelligent education products or solutions such as intelligent classrooms, intelligent lesson preparation, intelligent question answering, intelligent grading, personalized education, and intelligent campus management.

Besides, KG-powered intelligent products are being quickly accepted by industries such as government, security, transportation, energy, manufacturing, and many more. With the acceleration of industry transformation, enterprises are eager to manage and utilize knowledge to upgrade business operation and management. Baidu establishes Knowledge Development Platform based on knowledge graphs, NLP, search and recommendation technologies, to enable enterprises to produce, organize and use knowledge to upgrade business operation and management.

3.1.3 Trends and Prospects

1. Challenges

Major challenges that KG technology is facing rise from complex knowledge representation, quick knowledge acquisition and graph creation, and integrating knowledge into deep learning. Now relations in knowledge graphs are too simple to support complex applications. Acquisition and correlation of common sense, complex knowledge, and multimodal knowledge need to be strengthened. In addition, urgent issues need to be addressed before KG's further application, including how to acquire knowledge cheaply and quickly, how to create knowledge graphs, and how to use them in a highly efficient way. Another problem is that machines learn general rules rather than deeper knowledge from massive data. It is important and prospective to explore the learning mechanism and integrate knowledge into deep learning.

2. Future Directions

Challenges point the way forward. KG technology is heading towards complex knowledge representation, quick knowledge acquisition and graph creation, and integrating knowledge into deep learning.
Now considerable research is exploring the representation and linking of common sense, complex knowledge, multimodal knowledge, and even logical relations such as causality, addition, and contrast, to meet the need for knowledge reasoning in complex applications.
In addition, continuous research on mechanisms and methodologies for cheap yet efficient knowledge acquisition and graph creation, including few-shot learning and transfer learning, is an important guarantee for large-scale industrial application of KG.
Furthermore, using knowledge to increase the interpretability of deep learning and to eliminate deep learning's dependency on big data is beneficial to broader application of deep learning and further development of AI.

3. Application Focus

Shifted from general-purpose to industry-specific, simple to complicated, KG applications are also going from large-scale to small. Large-scale general-purpose applications, such as search engines, question answering, and recommendation systems, are relatively simple in that they have similar patterns, use simple knowledge representation methods, and are big-data dependent. Knowledge graphs that link together massive numbers of facts are their favorite way to represent knowledge and do work well in practice. However, industry-specific applications are totally different as they have diverse patterns and require intensive expert knowledge, but have limited data resources, which bring challenges along with opportunities for KG technology.

3.2 Language Understanding

Natural language understanding (NLU) is at the core of NLP and is the key to break through machine cognitive intelligence. In recent years, along with the rapid development of knowledge graph and deep learning technologies, there are many innovative work worth of notice in natural language semantic representation and understanding, cross-modal semantic understanding. NLU technology is widely used in search engines, recommendation systems, question answering, human-machine conversation, etc.

3.2.1 Technology Highlights

1. Semantic representation rises again and becomes a fundamental technology for NLU.

Semantic representation is the foundation of machine language understanding. One of the early approaches, one-hot representation embeds each word into a vector the length of the vocabulary, with a single 1 at its position in the vocabulary and the rest zeros. However, such a high dimensional sparse vector is not a good way to represent meaning, not to mention it is vulnerable to the curse of dimensionality. At NIPS 2001 (Conference on Neural Information Processing Systems), Yoshua Bengio et al. published *A Neural Probabilistic Language Model* where they used a three-layer neural network to build a language model and learn word embedding, i.e., to present each word with a low-dimensional, real-valued, dense vector. Mikolov further explored neural network language models and published the famous Word2Vec in 2013.

In 2018, Google proposed BERT for language representation pre-training, bringing awareness to the innovative paradigm of pre-training followed by fine-tuning as a key technique towards AI cognitive technology. BERT, the deep transformer language model, learns context-aware representations on huge amounts of unsupervised textual data, and solves various language understanding problems through the unified paradigm.

NLU research in China mainly focuses on knowledge integration and modelling methods. As shown in Fig. 3.5, Baidu released ERNIE 1.0, a knowledge-

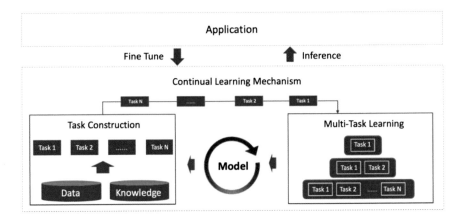

Fig. 3.5 Knowledge-enhanced continual learning pre-training framework

enhanced language representation model, and ERNIE 2.0, a continual pre-training framework for language understanding, in succession. ERNIE 1.0 learns semantic relations of the real world by modeling prior knowledge, such as entity concepts in massive data, and enhances the semantic representation of the model. On the basis of 1.0, ERNIE 2.0 proposes a framework for continuous learning of semantic understanding, which is used to learn knowledge of different dimensions such as lexical, grammar, and semantics in the corpus, and further enhances the effect of the model. ERNIE achieved the state-of-the-art results on 16 NLP tasks in both Chinese and English, and took things a level further by scoring the highest-ever score, the world's first 90, on GLUE (General Language Understanding Evaluation), a position previously held only by U.S. companies. Furthermore, it topped five tasks at International Workshop on Semantic Evaluation [27]. Researchers from Tsinghua University proposed to integrate structured knowledge graphs into pre-training, improving the effect by introducing the information in the knowledge graph into the language model, and published a series of papers in the field. A team from Alibaba incorporated text structure information into their pre-trained model, StructBERT. The Joint Laboratory of HIT and iFLYTEK Research constructed MacBERT using synonym information. The Zen model by HKUST (Hong Kong University of Science and Technology) explicitly took advantage of n-gram information. NEZHA by Huawei employed a proven-effective positional encoding scheme.

Other work focuses on domain-specific pre-training, multi-language understanding, language model compression, and more, besides general language understanding. Work on domain-specific pre-training includes ERNIE-Health and ERNIE-Law models constructed by Baidu on the basis of domain structural modeling task; BERT-civil and BERT-criminal, pre-training language models trained on legal documents by Tsinghua University and PowerLaw AI; and K-BERT by Tencent and Peking University, a knowledge-enabled language representation model with

Table 3.3 Major approach of semantic parsing

Tasks	Description	Research Institutions
Text-to-logical forms	Mapping text to logical forms such as first-order logical forms, lambda expressions, etc.	Universities
Text-to-graph or text-to-tree	Converting text to graphs or trees, such as AMR (abstract meaning representation) and UCCA (universal conceptual cognitive annotation) graphs.	Universities
Text-to- code	Parsing text into executable code such as SQL, Python and mathematical formulas	Universities and enterprises

medical knowledge graphs. On multi-language understanding, Microsoft Research Asia released Unicoder, which proposes bilingual pre-training technologies such as bilingual word granularity alignment and bilingual translation judgment and improves the effect of multilingual tasks. Work on language model compression includes DynaBERT by Huawei, a width- and depth-adaptive model obtained by first training a width-adaptive BERT and then distilling knowledge from the full-sized model to small sub-networks; MiniLM by Microsoft Research Asia, trained via task-agnostic distillation with attention transfer and value relation transfer; and AdaBERT by Alibaba, an adaptive BERT compression method that integrates Neural Architecture Search (NAS) with knowledge distillation to compress BERT into small models for specific tasks. Specially on dynamic inference, researchers from Tencent, Peking University, and Beijing Normal University jointly proposed FastBERT, a pre-trained model that uses a sample-wise adaptive mechanism to dynamically adjust the number of executed layers and speed up the inference. Baidu's data distillation method ERNIE-Slim ERNIE takes advantage of large-scale unsupervised data to transfer ERNIE's knowledge to lightweight models, which has been implemented in Baidu Search and achieved remarkable results.

2. Formal semantic parsing is still a hot topic of research.

Semantic parsing is an important research topic in NLU, parsing a natural language into a machine-computable formal language. Current mainstream methods of semantic parsing are shown in Table 3.3.

Parsers that convert text to logical forms or to graphs/trees are not yet ready for application and the research is mainly conducted at universities. However, text-to-code parsers can be directly applied together with knowledge graphs and attract attention from enterprises. Current algorithms for semantic parsing are supervised, i.e., they are learning from labeled or supervised data. So research on semantic parsing focuses on two aspects: datasets and parsing algorithms.

Research institutions in China have mainly worked on datasets of text-to-graph and text-to-tree tasks. Harbin Institute of Technology and Beijing Language and Culture University jointly built a Dataset of Chinese Semantic Dependency Parsing, and participated in [28]. Enterprises in China are more interested in text-to-code task. Relevant datasets include DuSQL by Baidu, Math23K by Tencent, and NL2SQL by Zhuiyi Technology.

The annually published papers on this topic by Chinese universities account for about 32.2% of the total, among which Tsinghua University, Chinese Academy of Sciences, Harbin Institute of Technology, and Shanghai Jiaotong University have the most publications.

3. There is extensive research on application-oriented language understanding technology.

Among the tasks that are widely needed in real-world applications, sentiment analysis is one of the hottest.

With the rapid development of internet platforms including e-commerce market-places and social media such as microblogs and communities, there emerges a lot of content with sentiments and emotions reflecting people's opinions and attitudes towards products, services, and events. Automatic mining and analyzing opinion content have been increasing in demand. As it is of commercial, social, and ideological importance, sentiment analysis becomes one of the most active fields in NLP research. Document-level sentiment analysis attaches a positive, negative, or neutral tag to a document. Sentence-level sentiment analysis uses such tags to classify sentences. Aspect-level sentiment analysis involves aspect extraction, entity extraction, and sentiment classification, yielding fine-grained sentiment information.

Harbin Institute of Technology proposed a representation learning method for document-level sentiment analysis, which first learns sentence-level representations based on CNN or LSTM and then models sentence representations and discourse relations using GRU (Gated Recurrent Unit) to obtain document-level representations. Tsinghua University proposed a method that encodes syntactic knowledge like part-of-speech into tree-structured LSTM to enhance representation of phrases and sentences, which achieves competitive results in sentence-level sentiment analysis. For aspect-level sentiment analysis, Harbin Institute of Technology developed a target-dependent LSTM model which incorporates target information as features and obtains state-of-the-art accuracy without using any syntactic parser or external sentiment lexicon.

4. Deep learning-driven cross-modal understanding becomes a new trend.

As multimedia such as images and videos get popular, cross-modal understanding has received more and more recognition from both academia and industry and is viewed as an important future direction of AI development.

Cross-modal understanding aims to enable machines to understand, express, and reason across language, vision, and speech. Typical tasks include Image Captioning, Video Captioning, Visual Question Answering, Video Question Answering, Visual Conversation, and Image-text Matching. For long video question answering, researchers from Zhejiang University proposed a multilayer attention encoder and a multimodal adversarial network-based decoder. Tsinghua University proposed a method of fusing multi-modal features to pass dynamic information across vision and language. It captures the high-level interactions between language and vision and significantly improves the performance of visual question answering. For image captioning, researchers at Chinese Academy of Sciences proposed a method of using scene graphs to integrate structured visual information into image caption models. Tencent AI Lab proposed Memory-Augmented Recurrent Transformer (MART) for video paragraph captioning, enhancing the transformer architecture with memory modules.

Recent research on cross-modal understanding focuses on multimodal representation learning. Unimodal representation learning has made remarkable progress in Computer Vision and NLP. Supervised pre-trained representation based on ImageNet has been widely used in tasks such as target detection and image segmentation, while large-scale unsupervised pre-training based on Transformer has brought significant improvement in language understanding and generation. Traditional multimodal representation learning methods fuse multiple unimodal representations via attention mechanism. Recently, multimodal representation learning based on large-scale multimodal aligned data has received lots of attention. Representative work includes VideoBERT and ViLBERT. They take word-embedding and visual features as input and models the joint representation characterizing the alignment across vision and language based on a multi-layer Transformer network. In China, Baidu proposed ERNIE-ViL, which integrates scene graph knowledge into the multi-modal pre-training process for the first time and learns cross-modal fine-grained semantic alignment. It has achieved the best performance in 5 typical multi-model tasks, such as Cross-Modal Retrieval, Visual Commonsense Reasoning, Visual Q&A, etc.. ERNIE-ViL, rank the first in the competition of Visual Common Sense Reasoning.

3.2.2   Application Highlights

Nowadays, NLU technology and applications have become popular in people's daily life. For example, we could ask smart speakers about the weather of the day, or scroll through the news feed apps on our phones in the morning. When encountering problems in our work or study, we use search engines to look for information and find answers. When shopping online, we read comments of different products and compare their pros and cons. NLU technology has also played an important role in the industrial transformation, such as enterprise search and recommendation enabling employees to easily find and use information and knowledge to work more effectively and creatively. And for industries as finance, healthcare and education, NLU technology is used to develop intelligent personalized financial service, intelligent clinical assistant, smart teaching assistant, etc. to help enterprises reduce cost and bring welfare to people. In these scenarios, intent understanding, text classification, semantic matching, sentiment analysis, cross-modal understanding, and other NLU technologies have played a key role.

Fig. 3.6 Natural language interaction with a smart speaker

1. Natural Language Interaction

In recent years, with the rapid development of speech technology and intelligent hardware, there is a strong customer demand for all kinds of intelligent devices. NLU-based interaction is most preferred by smart speakers. You may communicate with a smart speaker in a natural way that you talk to other people, asking it to play your favorite music, asking it about weather or stock market news, or having it remind you of different things as a personal assistant (Fig. 3.6).

Besides, in scenarios like driving or cooking where hands-free interaction is desired, natural language speech provides the most convenient and safest way for interaction. Baidu Map, with a "driving assistant" built in, answers users' voice queries for traffic information and route planning (Fig. 3.7).

Based on language intent understanding technology, the interaction and communication between human and machine are getting more natural and smoother.

2. Video Recommendation

With the continuous development of the Internet, the way people spread and access information has begun to shift from text to more efficient multimedia communication. As an important carrier of multimedia information, videos will see an explosive growth in the 5G era. Everyone can produce videos and access information through them. Cross-modal understanding technology can help users find videos that are most attractive to them out of a huge number of options, which significantly increases user stickiness to video platforms. Hence video recommendation has become a core product on different platforms.

3. Virtual Employee

Fig. 3.7 Driving Assistant in Baidu Map

Personalized virtual employee is developed to satisfy user's personal and intelligent
   demands in industries of healthcare, education, travel, news and finance. Virtual
   employee can recognize users' demands and give accurate answers through voice
   interaction. Virtual employee to some extent feels like "real" person with knowledge, thoughts and emotions.
In 2019, Shanghai Pudong Development Bank and Baidu jointly announced a new
   service called Virtual Employee "Xiao Pu". Xiao Pu is the first virtual employee
   of SPD Bank, providing 24-hour online service for clients. More clients enjoy the
   service, smarter Xiao Pu becomes.

3.2.3   Trends and Prospects

Today in the era of the Internet and intelligence, data, devices, and scenarios related
to language understanding and interaction are growing rapidly. People's need for
NLU technology is also increasing. More attention, education, research, and other

resources are being allocated to the NLP field. It's a prime time for NLU-related research. Future research may go in the following directions.

1. Unified NLU framework based on pre-training models and unlabeled data.

Since 2018, pre-trained language models have shown strong language understanding ability and achieved the state-of-the-art on a variety of NLU tasks. Issues like using massive unlabeled data to get better general-purpose pre-trained models, designing more reasonable model structures, and task-specific fine-tuning of pre-trained models will remain hot topics for some time.

2. Knowledge-enhanced language understanding

Natural language understanding involves not only understanding the literal meaning of language but also understanding the underlying knowledge and common sense. Therefore, modeling knowledge and common sense and integrating them into language models are of vital importance to language understanding. Currently Tsinghua University, Baidu, and other research institutions have done some work on knowledge integrated modeling and received desirable results. But the work is still in a primary stage. The modeling, integration, and use of knowledge, common sense, evaluation methods, and dataset construction are promising directions worthy of future endeavors.

3. Low-resource language understanding

For many application-oriented language understanding tasks, there are not so much labeled data. Low-resource language understanding is also an important research direction. Models and methods based on unsupervised learning, transfer learning, few-shot learning, meta learning, and multi-language learning may make the difference.

4. Text-visual cross-modal solutions

With rapid growth and wide application of NLP, KG, vision, deep learning and other AI technologies, cross-modal understanding technology has become more established and has even wider applications. Hardware such as AI chipsets, mobiles, and home appliances will further bring it into video understanding, smart home, and more applications in education, commerce, and healthcare.

3.3 Language Generation

Natural language generation (NLG) is among the key technologies in NLP field. NLG refers to theories and methods on how computers express and write like human by processing multimodal information and transforming it into natural language. NLG technology and applications will be introduced in this section.

3.3.1   Technology Highlights

Traditional NLG focuses on data-to-text generation and follows a three-stage pipeline:

1. Macro planning: including content selection and document structuring, i.e., deciding what content should be realized in the output and how it should be structured.
2. Micro planning: generating a detailed sentence specification and selecting appropriate referring expressions.
3. Surface realization: transforming the result of micro planning into grammatical and coherent text.

Some early NLG systems based on the traditional pipeline uses templates. As statistical approaches become mainstream, some steps in the traditional pipeline are replaced by data-driven methods.

With the rise of deep neural networks, LSTM, GRU, and other recurrent neural networks (RNNs) have shown extraordinary strength on natural language modeling. Based on RNNs, Seq2seq that encodes an input sequence and uses it as a condition for generating the output sequence becomes a mainstream approach for language generation. Most NLG models do not follow the traditional pipeline any more. After the input end and the output end are determined, deep neural networks can automatically complete input encoding, latent space transformation and output decoding in an end-to-end way. More efficient sequential modeling methods, such as the Transformer, further unleashed the potential of NLG to deal with long input and output sequences.

Since 2018, pre-training has become a default approach in NLP, as it takes advantage of a large amount of unlabeled data and provides good initialization parameters that are unlikely to be over-fitted to extensive downstream tasks.

Pre-training models such as MASS (MAsked Sequence to Sequence pre-training), UniLM (Unified Language Model), BART (Bidirectional and Auto-Regressive Transformers) have been proposed for a variety of NLG tasks and have raised the state-of-the-art. China's research institutions have become leaders instead of followers at this stage. For example, Baidu released the ERNIE-GEN model in May 2020, which achieved the state-of-the-art on five datasets of four NLG tasks [29] (Fig. 3.8). Compared to the existing models, ERNIE-GEN has the following innovations: (1) it alleviates the common exposure bias problem in language generation, through the filling generation mechanism and noise perception generation mechanism; (2) it proposes segment-by-segment learning method in units of semantic segment, together with the word-by-word learning method, as a dual-flow training to reduce the risk of local overfitting; (3) adopts a multi-segment and multi-granular sampling strategy, alleviating the problem that generation reduces the dependence of the encoding during long text training.

In 2020, introducing graph models into NLP has become a hot direction in the field. Baidu is the first to introduce graph neural network into the process of multi-

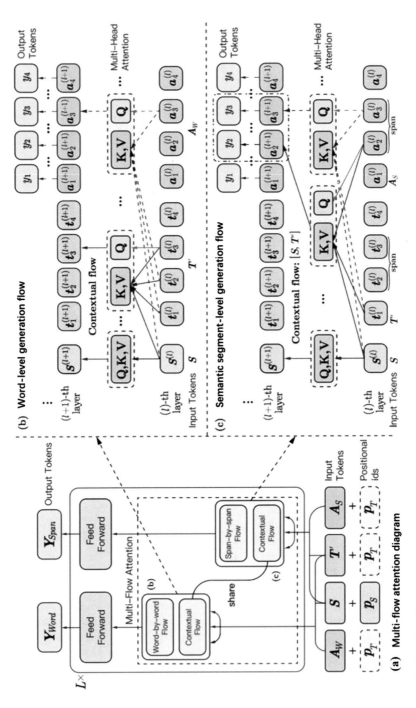

Fig. 3.8 ERNIE-GEN pre-training model

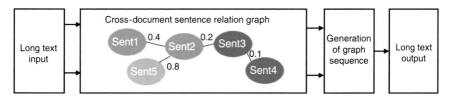

Fig. 3.9   Multi-document summary generation based on graph neural network

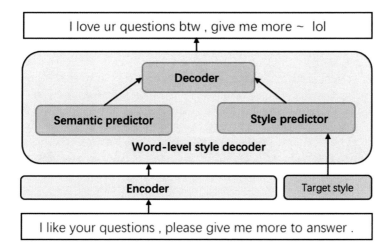

Fig. 3.10   Style conversion based on word-level precise control with non-parallel corpus

document summary generation. As shown in Fig. 3.9, the graph neural network can better represent the long text of multiple documents by modeling the relation between sentences in multiple documents. Based on this representation, combined with the Transformer model of the graph structure, the text generation effect can be significantly improved.

Another hot research direction of language generation is controllable language generation, which means that the generation results need to meet the given constraints. The study on controllable language generation is of great importance: first, from a practical perspective, meeting the given constraints helps the language generation algorithm adapt to the actual scenarios; second, from a technical perspective, once the language generation result was completely controllable, it would be closer to the way humans use language. On the basis of fluency and common sense, it is capable of appropriating language generation results according to interaction, and not relying on large-scale domain specific corpus. How to complete the language style transformation without parallel corpus is one of the basic technologies of controllable language generation. In 2020, Baidu proposed a style conversion method using non-parallel corpus to develop an algorithm with precise word-level control. As shown in Fig. 3.10, based on the text rewriting model, with the help of an independently trained style predictor, the style strength of each word is predicted, and the style of generated text is controlled based on the prediction.

3.3.2 Application Highlights

NLG has a wide range of practical applications, for its output usually directly reach users. This feature makes it a great challenge to the performance of language generation models because any error in generation may directly affect the user experience.

NLG was initially implemented to express the internal data and state of the computer system in natural language so that computers can interact with humans. The pursuit of intelligent human-computer interaction is rooted in people's ultimate expectation for computer and artificial intelligence. The well-known Turing test verified the intelligence of a machine through human-computer interaction. Although current NLG technology cannot achieve the barrier-free communication required by the Turing test, applications such as dialogue systems, intelligent customer service systems, and smart speakers have been relatively mature and capable of interacting with users under pre-defined scenarios.

In the scenario of human-computer interaction, there are two kinds of NLG applications:

1. Generating responses that satisfy users' needs conditioned on users' input. Corresponding tasks include human-machine conversation, automatic question answering, and others. A typical example of this application is smart speakers. In addition, this kind of application has given birth to a number of open platforms of interaction technology, for example, Xiao Ice by Microsoft, UNIT (Understanding and Interaction Technology) by Baidu, and WeChat Dialogue Open Platform by Tencent.
2. Rephrasing given text to generate appropriate results of required length and/or style. Corresponding NLG tasks include automatic text summarization, text style transfer, and others. For example, on Baidu App, users can choose to listen to summaries of the content they get via search or feeds in dialects, and they can even have the content narrated in a dialect, in male or female voice, or in whatever style they like.

In recent years, intelligent writing has become another trend in NLG application. Unlike human-computer interaction, writing is a form of production with important social value. Using AI to assist human writing will essentially enhance productivity.

In the scenario of intelligent writing, there are also two kinds of NLG applications:

1. Automatic writing: NLG algorithms handle the whole process of writing: material processing, text generation, and publication. It provides a good solution for writing time-sensitive content, such as earthquake alerts, or long-tail content.

2. AI-assisted writing: NLG algorithms provide inspirations and materials before writing, check and polish the content during writing, and even add summaries or headlines after writing.

Currently the media industry in China is undergoing an intelligent reform. Enterprises in China have open platforms of intelligent writing, for example, Baidu Brain Intelligent Writing Platform and Tencent DreamWriter.

In 2019, Baidu built an AI Media Lab jointly with People's Daily, using NLP and other AI technologies to create an intelligent "editorial team" to facilitate news production and improve human editors' efficiency.

3.3.3 Trends and Prospects

Challenges

NLG technology has been accelerating over the past 10 years, but challenges still remain.

1. NLG technology is not mature enough. NLG results are directly given to users who expect them to be comparable to human's. While NLG is progressing, some applications are not able to deliver expected performance.
2. It is difficult to evaluate NLG systems. As the same content can be expressed in various correct ways, there is no ideal method to evaluate the performance of NLG algorithms automatically. Automatic metrics are based on n-gram co-occurrence statistics, while labor-intensive and time-consuming human evaluations produce accurate results. The difficulty of evaluation not only raises the human cost of algorithm development, but also limits the efficiency and effectiveness of model training.
3. NLG algorithms are heavily dependent on labeled data. Although there are some approaches for learning NLG algorithms with few labeled samples, most well-performed algorithms rely on large amounts of labeled data. Such reliance will severely limit the use of NLG.

Technology Directions

NLG technology is not mature enough to meet the practical needs of many applications. Sequence modeling and pre-training for NLG are still important research directions.

1. Better general-purpose NLG models: The Transformer introduced in 2017 is now the mainstream model for NLG. Although the Transformer allows for much more parallelization and is better to capture long-distance dependencies than RNNs, researchers never stop exploring even better sequence modeling approaches.

Their focus will be on more parallel computing friendly methods and better approaches for variable-length sequence and long sequence modeling.

2. Better performance on specific NLG tasks: Although the pre-trained models and core models for NLG are for general purpose use, different NLG tasks have different features. Common NLG tasks include automatic question answering, human-computer conversation, automatic summarization, and others. More attention needs to be paid to features of specific tasks to improve performance. For example, for automatic summarization tasks, researchers need to pay special attention to how to improve coherence in the results, how to combine extractive and abstractive summarization, and how to better evaluate the results automatically.

In addition, other important directions of NLG include:

Cross-modal language generation: Traditional NLG deals with structured data/text, while current language generation applications may receive images, speeches, and videos as input. Better language generation requires better understanding and linking the multimodal input data.

Controllable language generation: Current applications need NLG to be more controllable and interpretable. Users expect to have more fine-grained control on style, content, and structure in generated text. Improving controllability and interpretability will further expand the application of NLG technology and also benefit less-supervised or even unsupervised language generation.

Application Focus

Current language generation applications include two types:

NLG task-oriented application systems. Typical examples include machine translation and human-computer conversation.

Scenario-oriented application systems that integrate multiple technologies including NLG. A typical example is intelligent writing systems.

The point of NLG industrial application is to provide technology solutions on the basis of in-depth analysis of various industrial scenarios and their pain points. Efforts may be made on automatic or semi-automatic writing for news reports, business data analysis, consulting reports, and other content, and AI-assisted writing that helps to discover hot topics, sort event threads, correct typing errors, polish the text, and censor the content, to enhance the overall productivity of the content business.

3.4 Intelligent Search

Intelligent search is an advanced form of information retrieval that provides users with fast and accurate multi-modal information. Intelligent search engines have become people's key access to information in daily life and work and one of the important fundamental technologies for new infrastructure construction in China. Over the past few years, China has seen progress and a series of breakthroughs in technology and the application of intelligent search.

3.4.1 Technology Highlights

A search engine is an information retrieval system designed to search the Internet for particular information in a systematic way. The technologies underlying search engines include web crawling, web data extraction, indexing, search ranking, natural language processing, and others. Traditional search engines, such as Baidu and Google in their early days, use keywords to retrieve large amounts of web pages on the Internet and present the most relevant and authoritative ones to users through link-based page importance measures. In recent years, Baidu, Google, and other search engines are turning to intelligent search which requires more natural interaction and more accurate and straightforward results. Greater challenges have been posed to semantic representation, matching and retrieval, and other underlying technologies of traditional search. New technologies such as deep question answering and machine reading comprehension have been introduced in intelligent search.

Semantic Matching

Semantic matching is one of the key techniques for intelligent search. It is used to measure the semantic similarity between user queries and web page titles, paragraphs, tables, images, or videos, and helps users find what they need in huge amounts of data. There are two types of earlier approaches of semantic matching to handle the synonymy and ambiguity issues in text based on semantic representation. The first is rule-based approaches that build semantic networks to represent meaning. The second is statistical approaches such as topic models. With the development of technology, statistical methods based on deep learning have gradually become the mainstream.

A classic early work is the Deep Structured Semantic Models (DSSM) [30] proposed by Jianfeng Gao at Microsoft, in which DSSM were trained on click-through data in a weakly supervised manner. However, based on the bag-of-words method, they were not good at modeling sequences. In 2014 Huawei Noah's Ark Lab proposed two related convolutional architectures, ARC-I and ARC-II, for sentence matching [31]. ARC-I used CNN to model local sequence patterns, while ARC-II used CNN to model the interaction between two sentences. Semantic matching methods proposed before ARC-II were all based on representation learning. ARC-II was the first interaction-based model. In 2016, Chinese Academy of Science proposed MatchPyramid [32] and Match-SRNN [33], which took interaction modeling to another level.

Enterprises such as Baidu is also aligned to the latest advance of semantic matching technology. SimNet [34], the semantic matching framework used in many applications in Baidu, involves a series of models of different network structures such as BOW, CNN, RNN, and MM-DNN. It adopts multi-grained modeling, simultaneous modeling char, unigram, bigram, collocation, and others, which has greatly improved the model performance and has been implemented in Baidu's search system. In addition, to better address the problem of long document modeling in information retrieval, Baidu proposed Reinforced Long Text Matching (RLTM) [35], an End-to-End neural ranking framework which involves two models trained jointly using reinforcement learning: a sentence selection model that selects query-relevant sentences in a long document and a sentence matching model that takes the query and the selected sentence as input and outputs a relevance score of the query and the document. On the basis of the self-attention-based Transformer proposed by Google, Sogou published the IR-Transformer in 2018, using multi-head attention for interactive matching. In 2019 Baidu developed the pre-training model ERNIE and the pre-training semantic matching model ERNIE-SIM which has been implemented in Baidu Search.

Semantic Retrieval

Semantic retrieval has also been vigorously developed in China. Traditional inverted-index retrieval is based on query term matching. Missing terms will cause semantically deviated results and explicit query rewriting/correction is needed. Semantic retrieval systems represent query terms as semantic vectors and have strong abilities of context-aware understanding and implicit query rewriting/correction. Semantic retrieval technology is being widely used in recommendation systems, product search, web search, and other scenarios.

Researchers from Alibaba proposed Enhanced Graph Embedding with Side information (EGES) [36] in 2018, using graph embedding to model the relations between users and items. Recently at SIGIR 2020, researchers from JD published the Deep Personalized and Semantic Retrieval (DPSR) [37] model with a two-tower architecture. They used a hybrid negative sampling approach to sample random negatives and batch negative and built an industrial-scale online serving system for embedding retrieval which brings a higher user conversion rate and a lower query rewrite rate.

Baidu started research and development of semantic retrieval in 2016, and released its large-scale webpage semantic retrieval model in 2018. Baidu's approach used two-tower architecture and effectively model semantics by fusing different semantic segmentation. This approach realized online real-time correlation return on one billion web pages. In 2019, Baidu has developed Semantic Retrieval 2.0 based on semantic matching pre-training technology (ERNIE-SIM), realizing semantic retrieval on ten-billion web pages.

Baidu Semantic Retrieval 2.0 uses a network structure with attention representation mechanism. The loss function is matrix-wise loss, and the optimization process is to stimulate the recall of positive samples from the candidate library. Thus, it is more suitable than the pair-wise optimization method in retrieval. Using multi-task learning, in addition to query and document correlation calculation, Baidu Semantic Retrieval 2.0 added a query-query semantic correlation generalization, and further enhanced the semantic robustness of semantic retrieval.

With the development of pre-training semantic understanding technology, semantic retrieval technology based on semantic indexing has inspired technological innovation on semantic retrieval, leading to the new round of search technology transformation.

Deep Question Answering and Machine Reading Comprehension

The popularity of intelligent devices with small screens or no screens poses new requirements to search engines. Instead of dozens of links, intelligent search engines should present on small-screen or no-screen devices a single accurate answer to each user query submitted in natural language. This is where deep question answering and machine reading comprehension come into play.

Deep question answering is the key technology for intelligent systems to present accurate results. End-to-End Open-Domain Question Answering with BERTserini published by Wei Yang et al. at NAACL 2019 and Dense Passage Retrieval for Open-Domain Question Answering by V. Karpukhin et al. at ACL 2020 show that deep question answering based on semantic representation and matching using open domain data is now able to understand users' questions and retrieve documents that meet users' needs from massive data. To extract fragments containing accurate answers from the retrieved documents, we need machine reading comprehension.

The task of machine reading comprehension (MRC) is to read a given text and then answer questions based on it. In recent years there have emerged a series of MRC models based on representation learning and attention mechanism, such as Match-LSTM, BiDAF, DCN, and R-NET. These models have performed pretty well on MRC datasets like SQuAD, whose questions can be answered using a single document, or even rivaled human performance. But many times, the system has to look at multiple documents to come up with an answer. So there come search-oriented MRC datasets MS-MARCO, SearchQA, and DuReader, where each question is paired with multiple candidate documents retrieved by search engines. Unlike looking for an answer in a single document, reading multiple documents that may contain multiple ambiguous and confusing answers is more challenging. Deep MRC models such as S-NET and V-NET [38] was proposed to address the challenges.

In large-scale industrial applications, neural network-based MRC models have much to improve in terms of generalization ability. A model is considered not so robust when it is over stable semantics-altering edits, or oversensitive to semantics-preserving edits, which can greatly impact users' experiences in real applications. In recent years, some research tried to address the problem of model robustness by means of generating adversarial samples and generating question paraphrases. A model's generalization ability refers to how well it can predict unseen data. It is one of the most important abilities of machine learning models and measures whether a model is really practical. Traditional evaluations normally use only one dataset with independent and identically distributed training and test data. However, in industrial applications, models need a strong generalization ability to handle real data that is not identically distributed as the training data. MRQA 2019, jointly organized by Stanford University, MIT, University of Washington, Princeton University, and other universities, set a machine reading shared task to test how well models can generalize beyond the datasets on which they were trained. Baidu proposed D-NET [39], a pre-training and fine-tuning framework for improving generalization of machine reading comprehension, and ranked first in the shared task. D-NET uses multiple pre-trained models to learn language features from different perspectives and corpora. With knowledge distillation technology, it is capable of realizing the semantic transfer from the teacher model to the student model based on ensemble learning, which brings the prediction superior to that of a single model.

3.4.2 Application Highlights

With the progress of search technology, traditional search engines have evolved into intelligent ones, showing the following three characteristics.

1. There is an increasing tendency for users to use natural language and multi-modal queries.

With the increasing popularity of smart phones, smart speakers, smart TV, smart in-car devices, and other technologies, instead of keyword search, many users tend to ask questions either in text or voice, or input images to search engines. As shown in Fig. 3.11, most user queries are in the form of natural language questions, which has posed greater challenges for accurate understanding of users' intent.

Intelligent search takes advantage of semantic representation and understanding technology, mapping information in different forms such as text, images, or videos into the same semantic space and aligning the representation of textual and visual features at a deeper semantic level to solve search requests that cannot be satisfied by term-matching.

Baidu's image search based on cross-modal understanding is now able to recognize over ten million articles, including over 20,000 plants and millions of cosmetics.

2. More efforts have been made to deliver accurate search results.

Unlike traditional search engines that provide top ten links on the first page, intelligent search engines present an accurate answer to a user's request at the top of the search page. For example, as shown in Fig. 3.11, a user wants to know whether Peppa is a male or female pig. The intelligent search system first analyzes the user query, then finds the part most relevant to the question in the retrieved documents, and finally presents the accurate answer on the top of other search

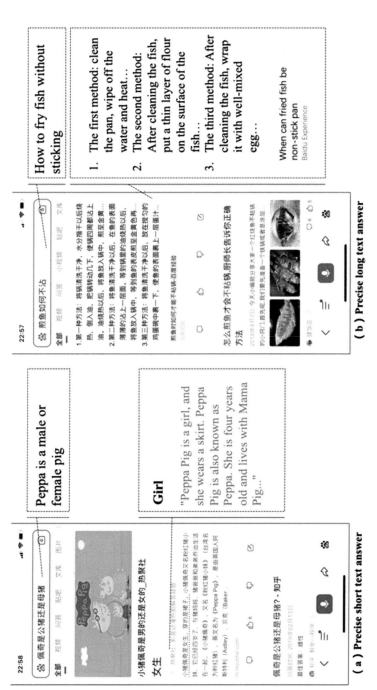

How to fry fish without sticking

1. **The first method:** clean the pan, wipe off the water and heat...
2. **The second method:** After cleaning the fish, put a thin layer of flour on the surface of the fish...
3. **The third method:** After cleaning the fish, wrap it with well-mixed egg...

When can fried fish be non-stick pan
Baidu Experience

(b) Precise long text answer

Peppa is a male or female pig

Girl

"Peppa Pig is a girl, and she wears a skirt. Peppa Pig is also known as Peppa. She is four years old and lives with Mama Pig..."

(a) Precise short text answer

Fig. 3.11 Natural language queries and accurate, multimodal search results

results. Intelligent search helps people to get more accurate and direct results and greatly improves the efficiency of information retrieval. Current search products in China, such as Baidu Search and Sogou Search both provide accurate search results now. According to Baidu, 58% of the queries on Baidu Search have been satisfied by its top 1 results [40]. That is to say, half of the queries that users entered into Baidu Search have been directly given only one answer.

Intelligent search engines present search results in a variety of forms other than text, such as tables, images, audios, and videos. In the era of mobile Internet, the cost of user content production is getting lower. More small and short videos are emerging. With the launch of 5G commercialization, an increasing proportion of search results are videos.

Overall, intelligent search engines provide more natural interaction and more accurate and direct results than traditional ones that return a couple of candidates based on keyword search [41]. Baidu and Google are leading the Chinese and English search market respectively, way ahead of other enterprises in terms of market share and search result satisfaction. In addition, a number of third-party evaluations have shown that the smart speakers of Baidu and Google have much better question answering performance than their competitors.

3.4.3   Trends and Prospects

Despite the breakthroughs in intelligent search, there are still many problems, including inaccurate cross-modal representation, lack of inference ability, and low robustness of models. Future research on intelligent search should focus on unified cross-modal representation, inference, and model robustness.

1. Unified cross-modal question answering
2. Inferable question answering and machine reading comprehension
3. Robust question answering

Enterprises that have cloud computing businesses have started to output the ability of intelligent search to enterprise users via cloud services. One of the typical applications is enterprise search that helps employees and clients with fast and accurate information retrieval. Unlike personal user products, enterprise search needs to be customizable so that the intelligent search system can adapt to the business data of different enterprises. Now only Amazon and Baidu provide fully open customizable question answering. In general, cloud-based question answering services are still in their infancy and will be a future focus of cloud service providers.

3.5 Machine Translation

Since the beginning of the twenty-first century, the acceleration of globalization and the increasing frequency of international exchanges arouse an urgent need for efficient cross-language communication and cooperation. Language barriers have become a major impediment to globalization. In recent years, with the progress of artificial intelligence technology, machine translation research has made great breakthroughs. Neural Machine Translation became mainstream as the quality of translation leaped to a new height. Meanwhile, great progress has also been made in the research and application of cross-modal translation. With the continuous increase of application scenarios, machine translation plays an increasingly important role in cross-cultural, economic, and political exchanges.

3.5.1 Technology Highlights

1. Neural machine translation has become mainstream.

In recent years, the rapid progress of machine translation is mainly driven by deep learning. Neural network based end-to-end translation models are able to learn language representations at a deeper level and make better use of context to produce better translations. In 2014, Bahdanau, Cho, and Bengio proposed a neural network translation model [42] by jointly learning to align and translate. Its main ideas such as bidirectional encoder and attention mechanism have become important components of neural translation models. The same year, Sutskever et al. proposed a LSTM-based Sequence-to-Sequence translation model [43]. Through these models, neural networks showed their potential for translation. But problems such as out-of-vocabulary words left untranslated and slow decoding due to model complexity impeded the large-scale application of neural machine translation.

Baidu took a lead in breaking through the internationally recognized challenges by proposing a neural network translation model with rich statistical features. This NMT model has several advantages as follows: first, by integrating features of large-scale phrase table, it overcomes the shortcomings of low vocabulary coverage and improves the translation quality of out-of- vocabulary words significantly; second, by adding features of language model and translation text length, the translation fluency is improved dramatically and the omission is solved by rewarding the decoder to generate longer and more complicated translation; furthermore, it is adopted with a fast decoding algorithm based on priority queue, reducing the search space greatly of traditional columnar decoding. All these technological breakthroughs have made possible large-scale industrial application of neural machine translation [44]. In May 2015, Baidu released the world first online neural machine translation system, while Google proposed its neural machine translation system in September 2016 and the attention-based

Transformer in 2017. The Transformer model completely gets rid of the network structure of RNN or CNN, and quickly becomes the mainstream network structure because of its excellent performance. It is applied not only on machine translation, on other tasks in NLP, but also on speech and CV tasks. The development of NMT has accelerated ever since. Major Internet companies in and outside of China started to adopt neural translation systems as their primary translation system. In recent years, Baidu, Alibaba, Tencent, Sogou, and iFLYTEK have all been ranked the first on multiple tracks, demonstrating the overall level of machine translation research in China.

2. Cross-modal translation combining speech and vision technology becomes a hot topic in research and application.

With the growing popularity of intelligent devices, voice and visual interactions are more welcomed as convenient and efficient ways of communication. Simultaneous machine translation that combines with speech technology is facing a dilemma between translation quality and latency. Baidu, Alibaba, Tencent, iFLYTEK, Sogou, Youdao, and other companies in China have been exploring in this field and made great breakthroughs in technology. For example, Baidu proposed a series of innovative methods, including a simultaneous translation model with integrated anticipation and controllable latency, an information unit-driven context-aware translation model, a translation model with joint textual and phonetic embedding, and an interactive learning model that performs speech recognition and translation simultaneously. Such methods have overcome the challenges met by the traditional machine translation technology. Based on these innovations Baidu released the first speech-to-speech simultaneous translation system [45]. At ACL 2020, Baidu organized the first workshop on automatic simultaneous translation jointly with Google, Facebook, Tsinghua University, and University of Pennsylvania, released a large-scale Chinese-English simultaneous machine translation data set, and held the world's first machine simultaneous translation evaluation. Now simultaneous translation systems developed by various companies have been widely used at international conferences.

3. There is a huge market for multilingual machine translation.

In the era of globalization, there is a huge market for multilingual machine translation. In 2013, China announced the One Belt One Road Initiative that seeks collaboration with 65 countries and regions. By August 2019, 136 countries and 30 international organizations have signed 195 cooperation documents with China, in 111 languages. The demand for multilingual machine translation has increased dramatically.

Due to the uneven distribution of language resources, multilingual machine translation is facing a problem of data scarcity. Data augmentation, multilingual joint modeling, reinforcement learning, and transfer learning have become hot topics in the research of multilingual translation. As early as 2015, Baidu proposed a multi-task learning model for multilingual machine translation [46], as shown in Fig. 3.12. By building a shared encoder on the source language side, a unified

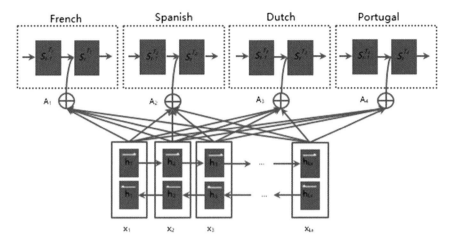

Fig. 3.12 Multi-task learning model for multilingual machine translation

semantic representation of the source language is established, without needing to model each language pair separately when translating multiple language. The number of encoders is reduced to 1/N of the traditional method (N is the number of languages). This method breaks bottlenecks of traditional method, such as knowledge sharing, complicated system construction and high cost, and improves the multilingual translation quality and deployment efficiency. Later Google proposed a multilingual translation system enabling zero-shot translation, training many languages jointly and sharing the encoder, decoder, and parameters across all languages. In addition, back translation is also an effective method for data augmentation.

Mainstream online translation systems, in or outside of China, all support multilingual translation. For example, Baidu Translate supports 203 languages, while Google Translate supports 108, Youdao Translator 107, Microsoft 74, Sogou 61, iFLYTEK 59 and Tencent 17.

3.5.2 Application Highlights

Thanks to the progress of machine translation technology, the quality of translation has been constantly improving, and the translation market is booming. Tech giants in and outside of China have increased their investment in machine translation. More language service providers begin to accept and use machine translation to improve efficiency. According to 2019 China Language Service Industry Development Report, the total value of global language services is approaching $50 billion US dollars for the first time. Fifty-three percent of the language service providers surveyed are largely satisfied with current machine translation quality. Machine translation has entered the stage of large-scale industrial application.

Currently there are three types of machine translation service providers. First, tech giants, including Google, Microsoft, Facebook, Amazon, Twitter, Yandex, Naver, Baidu, Tencent. Baidu has provided translation API service since 2012 and over 400,000 developers and enterprises have developed their own applications. So far, the number of characters translated everyday on Baidu Translate reaches 100 billion. Second, newly emerging machine translation startups such as NewTranx, Atman, and NiuTrans, which are focusing on domain-specific machine translation, providing customizable services to enterprises. Third, traditional language service providers which have established machine translation departments to reduce labor costs and increase efficiency, for example, TransPerfect, Lionbridge, LanguageLine Solution, SDL, Pactera, Transn, and GTCom.

Now machine translation services are not only running on PC, but also on a wide variety of terminals such as mobile phones and portable translation machines. Besides text, they also translate speech, images and video. Speech translation that allows voice input saves users from typing in source texts and is often used when travelling abroad or attending conferences. Instant camera translation and AR translation are widely used to translate menus, street signs, animation, and more. In terms of industrial application, machine translation providers focus more on customizable domain-specific translation, providing high-quality service by large-scale pre-training and domain-specific fine-tuning.

Machine translation also has great application potential in language learning, cross-border e-commerce, cultural exchange, and even military defense security.

3.5.3 Trends and Prospects

As our knowledge about the learning and translation mechanisms of the human brain is very limited, machine translation is still in the stage of symbol transformation, a long way from understanding and representing the nature of language. As for cross-model translation, which has a big market, current systems are based on a simple combination of speech, language, and vision technology and are facing error propagation and quality-efficiency dilemmas. What's more, it is difficult to build high-quality translation systems for low-resource languages and domains.

In general, a future direction is to explore a unified framework for multilingual, multi-domain, and cross-modal machine translation to break the bottlenecks such as data scarcity, language complexity, and data heterogeneity.

First, knowledge-based machine language. Current machine learning methods learn general, superficial rules from large amounts of data. Translation is not merely conversion between languages. Behind languages are cultures, histories, and civilizations. Without background knowledge, common sense, and world knowledge, the translation will fail to deliver the sense and flavor of the source text. To build knowledge-based machine translation models is an important and cutting-edge research topic.

Secondly, cross-modal machine translation. Current mainstream cascade systems feature loose coupling and face the problem of error propagation. Deeper integration of machine translation, speech technology, and vision technology will help build end-to-end translation systems with strong error tolerance/correction ability and low latency.

Thirdly, low-resource machine translation. Multilingual and multi-domain machine translation are facing the problem of data scarcity. More efforts are needed on multilingual parallel dataset construction, data augmentation, transfer learning, and multilingual joint modeling.

Machine translation has entered the stage of large-scale industrial application. The continuously increasing translation quality has resulted in more and more recognition. For common users, machine translation has become more useful in language learning, overseas travelling, and shopping. For enterprises, machine translation models based on large-scale pre-training plus domain-specific fine-tuning can help them go global. For government sectors, machine translation systems independently developed in China can help them with timely information acquisition, political, economic, cultural communication, and national security.

3.6 Dialogue System

Driven by NLP, KG, big data and deep learning, human-computer conversational interaction has seen great progress. There are two types of dialogue systems: task-oriented and open domain. A task-oriented dialog system is designed to accomplish specific goals, while an open domain system models open-domain conversation without specific goals, focusing more on establishing close connections with users by satisfying their needs for communication.

In recent years, research institutions and enterprises in and outside of China have paid great attention and effort towards the technology and application of dialogue systems and have made a series of progress and breakthroughs.

3.6.1 Technology Highlights

Task-Oriented Dialogue

1. Using few-shot learning, data augmentation, transfer learning, and other techniques to improve the cold start of task-oriented dialogue systems

Task-oriented dialogue systems are highly dependent on machine learning, but it is difficult to get enough training data for every task. Few-shot learning, data augmentation and transfer learning are trying to reduce machine learning's dependence on data by increasing data use efficiency and data diversity respectively. Few-shot learning [47, 48] is to train a model on several related tasks so that it can generalize well to unseen tasks with just a few examples. Data augmentation, either transformative or generative [49, 50], is to add more variation to the training data to improve a model's generalization ability and robustness, and prevent overfitting on small datasets.

Transfer learning is also an effective method to alleviate the lack of training data in task-oriented dialogue systems. By transferring knowledge from the source task to the target task, the problem of lacking labeled corpus can be solved. For example, how to change the train ticket reservation system to an air ticket reservation system when the data of airlines is limited. In this case, the two fields have high similarity and overlap in intent and slot. Transfer learning can greatly reduce the amount of data in the target field required in this case. Of course, transfer learning can be used in other fields and other dimensions. The main algorithms used in transfer learning include parameter sharing and model sharing.

2. End-to-end task-oriented dialogue system

A traditional task-oriented dialogue system consists of several components, including dialogue understanding, state tracking, dialogue policy, and others. Each component works in order, resulting in high dependence on data, non-sharing of features, and error aggregation. The end-to-end task-oriented dialogue model that can effectively avoid these problems, has gradually become a new technology trend.

(a) Integrated dialogue model of multiple methods: It is difficult to build a single model independently to handle the entire dialogue process. In 2016, Wen et al. proposed a method of fusing multiple models to realize end-to-end learning, using same data model all tasks at the same time, resulting in reducing the complexity of the model and to a certain extent reducing the dependence of pure end-to-end learning on large amounts of data.

(b) Dialogue model based on reinforcement learning: This end-to-end training framework was proposed in 2016 by Zhao et al. It jointly models all tasks, except NLG task, and accelerates the learning by combining supervised learning and reinforcement learning. Li et al. improved Zhao's framework in 2017, optimizing problem types, robustness, and user Q&A interruption, so that the reinforcement learning model can better handle changes in task-oriented dialogues.

(c) Dialogue models based on large-scale pre-training: Models based on large-scale pre-training are also applied to end-to-end task-oriented dialogue modeling, such as GPT-2 (Fig. 3.13). With powerful memory and prior knowledge brought by pre-training, these models can greatly improve the performance of task-oriented dialogue. It is capable of direct modeling with a single model. The pre-trained features can ease the need for large-scale training data and make it easy to transfer. Compared with the traditional

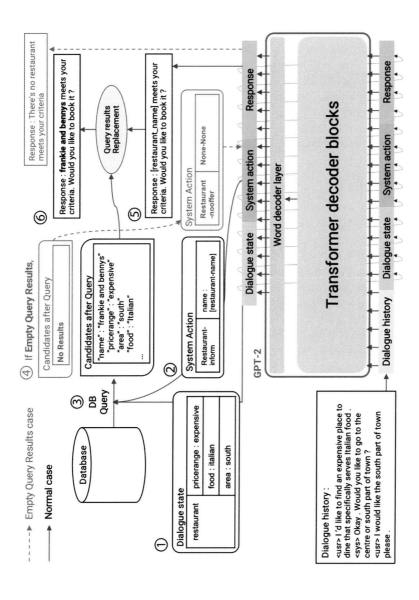

Fig. 3.13 End-to-end dialogue model based on GPT-2

pipeline dialogue model, these generative end-to-end dialogue systems based on pre-trained networks have not only made considerable progress in analytics, but also significantly improved their generation.

Open-Domain Dialogue System

Building an open-domain dialogue system that can talk about anything is one of the most challenging tasks. It has always been believed to be an ultimate goal for NLP or even AI. There have been rule-based or template-based [51], retrieval-based [52], and sequence generation-based open-domain dialogue systems. In recent years, with the popularization of large-scale neural network models, generative models have shown significant performance improvement, especially for multi-turn dialogue. Due to its flexibility and huge potential, generative approach has gained lots of attention.

1. Generative models based on large-scale deep neural network

With the booming of deep learning in recent years, there emerged the Transformer, BERT, ERNIE, XLNet, Roberta, and other generative models. They have achieved remarkable results on a variety of NLP tasks. Recently, Microsoft proposed the DialoGPT model with 762M parameters. Researchers from Baidu proposed PLATO, a pre-trained dialogue generation model with discrete latent variable and 1.6B parameters. Meena by Google, which has 2.6B parameters, scored high on SSA (Sensibleness and Specificity Average). Blender by Facebook, the 9.4B parameter model blending multiple skills for conversation, outperformed other approaches in multi-turn dialogue in terms of engagingness and humanness measurements. The increased number of parameters have resulted in increased learning ability and improved performance. Among the above models, Baidu's PLATO model adopts a multi-stage learning method. It firstly learns without latent variables, then adds latent variables, and simultaneously trains two models of Diversified Generation and Evaluation. This learning method results in breakthroughs in training efficiency, dialogue suitability, and personification (Fig. 3.14).

2. Knowledge or latent variable guided dialogue generation

Early dialogue systems based on RNN Seq2Seq models are likely to generate safe responses. Many approaches have been proposed to solve this problem, which can be categorized into two types. One is to introduce external knowledge to help response generation. A common way to do so is to automatically or manually select response-relevant knowledge candidates in a dialogue turn or a complete dialogue session and add them to training data. During training, the model can either use an attention mechanism for implicit knowledge selection [53] or explicitly select appropriate knowledge from candidates and feed them to the decoder for response generation [54]. The other approach is to model the one-to-many mapping between utterances and appropriate responses based on

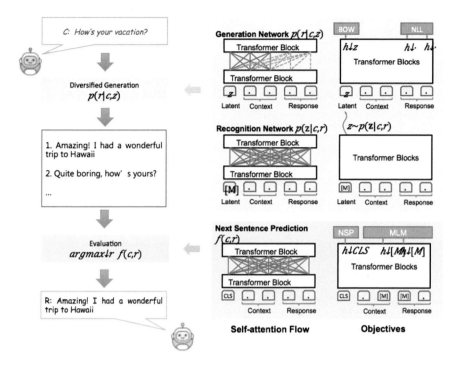

Fig. 3.14 The architecture of Baidu's PLATO model

conditional variational autoencoders (CVAE) [55]. The CVAE framework can learn from dialogue data continuous or discrete latent variables that encode abstract information such as dialogue acts and sentence patterns. With more detailed modeling of dialogue, models can generate more informative and diverse responses.

Tsinghua University proposed a Commonsense Knowledge Aware Conversational Model (CCM), which promotes dialogue understanding and generation effects by introducing a large-scale common sense knowledge base. In the process of introducing knowledge, the model proposes two new graph attention mechanisms, as shown in Fig. 3.15: The static graph attention mechanism encodes the retrieved graph to improve the semantics of the problem and help the system fully understand the problem; the dynamic graph attention mechanism will read each knowledge graph and its triples, and use the semantic information of the graph and triples to make a more reasonable response. The automatic evaluation and manual evaluation show that compared with the current state-of-the-art models, CCM can generate more reasonable and informative responses.

3. Dialogue management mechanism

In order to improve the coherence and logic of multi-turn dialogue, researchers proposed to introduce explicit dialogue management to better control the multi-

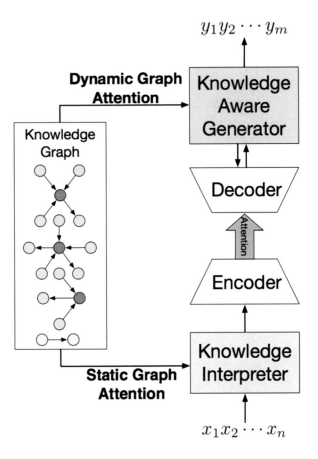

Fig. 3.15 The architecture of CCM model

turn dialogue flow. There are three major types of approaches: (1) models manage the responses through the planning of sentence-level latent variables, phrases, keywords, or dialogue acts [56]; (2) models plan multi-turn dialogue by introducing session-level goals [57]; (3) policy models plan responses through random walks and node selection on dialogue graphs that determine the dialogue flow [58].

The dialogue management technology based on knowledge graphs has gradually attracted attention. Researchers have tried to introduce knowledge graphs to support dialogue management, including topic sequence planning and in-depth chats around topics, and proposed a dialogue system based on knowledge graphs and hierarchical reinforcement learning framework (knowHRL), which includes the selection of multi-granular response guidance information and response generation. As shown in Fig. 3.16, the decision-making module of the reinforcement learning framework consists of three layers: (1) the upper layer is responsible for planning a coherent, diverse and sustainable chat topic by selecting entity nodes in the knowledge graph; (2) the middle layer is responsible for selecting a node from the neighbors of the entity node as a topic-facet; (3) the

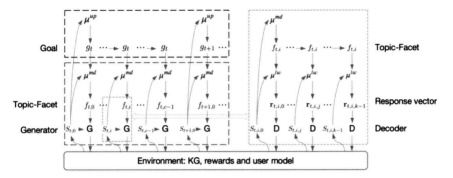

Fig. 3.16 The architecture of KnowHRL model

lower layer is responsible for selecting a response vector. The experimental results verify the effectiveness of the KnowHRL model under multiple indicators, including topic coherence, user interest consistency, and knowledge accuracy.

Other hot research topics include dialogue evaluation, emotional dialogue, personalized dialogue, among others. International companies such as Facebook, Microsoft, Amazon, and Google have been working in this field for a long time. Chinese enterprises including Baidu, Tencent, and Alibaba are racing to catch up.

3.6.2 Application Highlights

Task-oriented dialogue systems are relatively mature and have been used in a variety of scenarios such as intelligent customer service, smart speakers, and intelligent in-car devices, covering a wide range of industries including telecommunication, finance, airline, education, automobile, and others. Different from task-oriented dialogue systems, open-domain dialogue systems are mainly used as a catch-all solution in human-computer interaction. The remainder of this section will concentrate on the industrial application of task-oriented dialogue systems.

1. Intelligent customer service

The customer service market in China is still growing. According to the Report of Market Prospective and Investment Opportunities Analysis on China Call Center Industry (2020–2025) from Qianzhan Industry Research Institute, the total number of full-time customer service employee is about five million, the market scale of customer service industry is about 400 billion yuan, and the intelligent customer service market will reach 50–80 billion yuan.

Table 3.4 Intelligent customer service products and potential of dialogue systems

Product	Description	Application scenario	Potential of dialogue systems
Intelligent IVR	A system that enables users to communicate with customer service bots via voice rather than keyboard	Inbound calls to a call center	Voice interaction
Customer service assistant	A bot that provides customer service staff with knowledge and scripts based on users' utterances to reduce the response time	Script recommendation for call center agent systems; service inquiry in multi-channel customer service	Identifying users' intent and key information in human-human dialogue for service or script retrieval
Intelligent calling system	A bot that makes phone calls to and communicates with users via voice	Simple calls for satisfaction survey, questionnaire survey, service notification, etc.	Voice interaction
Online customer service	A bot that communicates online with users 24/7 via voice or text	Customer support on multiple channels such as web, H5, WeChat, other apps, etc.	Intelligent dialogue service, knowledge base management
Intelligent training	A bot that plays the role of users, communicates with customer service staff via voice, and scores their responses	Customer service training and assessment	Full-process intelligent dialogue support
Intelligent quality control	A system that conducts quality control over all communication data between customer service staff and users, and improves data value through business data mining	Call center customer service team leader or quality control center	Identifying users' intent and key information in human-human dialogue, detecting quality control points

At present, customer service provided online and via call centers is going intelligent, where dialogue systems have roles to play. Table 3.4 lists some products of intelligent customer service and describes the potential of dialogue systems.

2. Consumer Applications

Consumer voice interaction systems, including mobile voice assistants, wearable assistants like hearables, intelligent TVs, intelligent storytellers, and intelligent in-car devices. According to 2020 China's AIoT Industry Report released by iResearch, the consumer AIoT market was valued at RMB 175.3 billion in 2018, accounting for 68% of the total IoT market. Hardware manufacturers, Internet companies, and AI companies are all aiming at consumer intelligent interactive terminals for their high market potential. Behind intelligent terminals is a broader ecosystem, for example, an open voice platform, a voice operating system, or an audio/video content ecosystem.

Voice assistants are the voice control program for various intelligent terminals, following users' voice commands to complete various tasks. Current voice enabled consumer hardware falls in four categories: smart home devices, children's products, wearable devices, and in-car devices (Table 3.5).

In these application scenarios, smart speakers as the entrance to smart life are considered to be very promising by smart home practitioners. According to 2020 China's Intelligent Voice Industry Report published by iResearch, smart speaker shipment in China reached 72 million by the end of 2019. With an urban household penetration rate of 20%, which is close to the penetration rate of smart phones in 2012, smart speakers have crossed the first threshold of popularity.

In the automobile industry, dialogue systems have been implemented in vehicle systems, enabling voice interactive control over cars. This implementation has created a relatively mature industry chain. Technology companies flock to invest in the Intelligent Internet of Vehicles (IoV), providing service to vehicle manufacturers. New market opportunities have also emerged for voice-enabled intelligent in-car devices such as rear-view mirrors and mobile holders. In map and navigation apps, voice interaction ability has become a must. The hands-free and eyes-free interaction is easy to use and effective in minimize distraction while driving (Figs. 3.17, 3.18, and 3.19).

3. Office Applications

Intelligent office aims at improving efficiency and user experience. AI-empowered office products have become increasingly popular. Dialogue systems are playing the role of office secretary in various office scenarios (Table 3.6).

3.6.3 Trends and Prospects

Despite the recent progress, dialogue systems remain the biggest challenge in NLP.

Inference Computing: Current dialogue systems are weak at knowledge-based inference computing. Even the largest model now fails to deal with inferences like, "It's raining so there will be a traffic jam later" and "you are 30 now, so you must have a job."

Dialogue Understanding: Multi-turn and multi-intent dialogue understanding remains a problem that is not fully solved. An input utterance may have different meanings in different contexts. A user may have more than one intent when uttering a sentence. In addition, a user's manner of speaking, personality, and mood, and even the time of a conversation, have an impact on the understanding of the utterance. Further research is needed on modeling the context and various related factors to fully understand users' intent. Research on cross-model understanding of dialogue, images, and motions has been put on the agenda in recent years.

Table 3.5 Voice assistant products and typical cases

Hardware	Product	Description	Typical case
Smart home device	Smart speaker	• Voice/screen interaction • Weather forecast • Music playback • Smart home control	Xiaodu smart speaker, Tmall genie, XiaoAI speaker
	Smart TV	• Voice control for on-off switching, channel switching, content search, volume, etc.	Mi TV, Changhong AI3.0, Skyworth 55Q6A
	Smart STB	• Voice control • Video search • Weather/stock information • Music playback	Mi box, Penguin Aurora, Skyworth π box
Children's product	Companion robot	• Small in shape • Voice interaction • Educatoinal resource built-in • Companionship via converation	ZIB robot, Alpha egg, Pudding robot, Little fish, YEXBOT
	Smart storyteller	• Small in shape • Voice interaction • Story telling • Music playback	Mi bunny, Alpha egg, 360 storyteller, Alilo bunny
	Smart learning machine	• Tablet or robot • Voice/screen interaction • Rich learning resource built-in	Xiaodu smart display, OK learning machine, iFLYTEK learning machine
Wearable	Bluetooth hearables	• Bluetooth • Voice control • Zero button	Xiaomi, UBL, Huawei, Jabra
	Smart watch	• Voice or touch control • Information access	Xiaomi, Huawei, 360, OKii
	Smart translator	• Hand-held • Voice interaction • Machine translation	iFLYBUDS, iFLYTEK translator, Sogou translator, Sogou recording pen
Car & in-car device	Intelligent vehicle system	• Internet of vehicle • Voice control • Music playback • Web search	Baidu IOV OS, Banma system, Pateo, AliOS
	Smart Mobile holder	• Voice interaction • Bluetooth	Xiaodu AI voice Car phone holder
	Smart rearview Mirror	• Mirror screen • Navigator • Driving recorder • Voice control	DuMirror, Mi smart RearView Mirror, Blackview
Mobile phone	Mobile system assistant	• System-level voice assitant • Voice wake-up	Siri, Oppo Breno
	In-APP voice assistant	• In-app voice assistant • Voice wake-up	Baidu map voice assistant

Fig. 3.17 Voice Interaction on Baidu Map

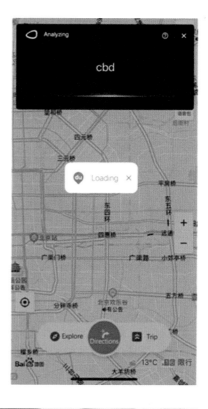

Fig. 3.18 Voice Interaction with Intelligent Vehicle System

Domain Adaptation: It is hard to collect domain-specific dialogue data and build domain-specific dialogue systems. On one hand, how to efficiently get labeled multi-turn dialogue data is an urgent problem. On the other hand, how to make full use of

Fig. 3.19 Baidu's DuMirror

Table 3.6 Dialogue systems in office scenarios

Office scenario	Dialogue system
Intelligent administration	Employees can communicate with an AI administrative assistant via voice or text instant messaging. It facilitates a series of processes like attendance and leave management, expense claim, and others. A self-service and simple administrative process will improve the job satisfaction and work efficiency of employees
Intelligent question-answering	Sometimes the staff in HR, IT, administration, or even finance will have to take over the tasks of customer service to answer their colleagues' questions about company rules and regulations. An intelligent question-answering assistant with loads of documents as its knowledge base can reduce the workloads of functional departments and improve their work efficiency and satisfaction
Meeting room reservation	Meeting room reservation is no longer just about application and approval, but inquiry, booking, check-in, and check-out anytime and anywhere through a conversational assistant. There is no need to confirm the time of meeting with every participant; the AI assistant will coordinate the meetings through conversation and send out invitations. During the meetings, the AI assistant can make remote phone calls and generate meeting minutes
Intelligent task management	For traditional task management, information confirmation is tedious, time-consuming, and easy to forget. Intelligent task assistants are used to help employees push forward the progress, collect information, and make reports. They can also act as personal secretaries that remind employees of their tasks and help organize their work

transfer learning and large-scale unsupervised pre-training to allow models' self-adaptation to new domains is a direction worth exploring.

Chapter 4
Trends and Prospects

4.1 Challenges

An inter-discipline of linguistic, computer science, and cognitive psychology, NLP is one of the most challenging subjects in AI. In recent years, NLP has been widely applied in various scenarios, which has posed new challenges to NLP. Generally speaking, current breakthroughs in NLP were brought by big data and deep learning. In particular, it was thanks to the progress of pre-training that large-scale unlabeled data could be used to improve the understanding ability of models. However, over-dependence on big data, interpretability, lack of deep understanding and reasoning, and low tolerance to noises remain problems for models.

Major challenges before NLP include:

1. In terms of knowledge representation and acquisition, acquiring and linking simple facts are not enough to support complicated cognitive activities such as analysis, understanding, decision-making, planning, and others. More efforts are needed on acquiring common sense, complex knowledge and multimodal knowledge, sorting out cause-effect relations and time-sequential relations among them, and representing them explicitly or implicitly.

2. Machines are not able to well-learn and make full use of knowledge. Machines learn general rules, such as whether two words often occur together, rather than deeper knowledge from massive data. In addition, models cannot fully use existing linguistic knowledge and entity knowledge to conduct deeper understanding and reasoning. Building self-learning and knowledge-integrated models is an important and frontier topic.

3. Machines do not have self-awareness and cannot judge whether their acts or decisions are correct or logical. Their results are weakly interpretable. Introducing knowledge or other interpretable models on the basis of existing deep learning models remains a topic worth investigating.

4. Data-driven models mechanically learn superficial patterns from massive data without real understanding. Randomly adding distractors with similar patterns

Chinese Academy of Engineering, *The Development of Natural Language Processing*, https://doi.org/10.1007/978-981-16-1986-1_4

into the training data will impact their robustness. How to improve models' tolerance to noise and robustness is of vital importance.

4.2 Future Directions

NLP will advance along the following tracks.

1. Improving complex knowledge acquisition, knowledge representation learning, knowledge inference for low-cost, transferable KG construction, and continuous incremental learning.
2. Pre-training is expected to develop further for low-resource language translation and cross-modal understanding.
3. Low-shot learning is expected to make new breakthroughs. Data scarcity is a common problem. Few-shot learning, transfer learning, and multi-task learning will move forward to alleviate the problem.
4. NLP based on semantic parsing and knowledge will be in big demand. Deep learning based models are usually a black box with output that is difficult to interpret. How to take advantage of traditional syntactic and semantic parsing, rules, and knowledge to achieve language understanding and interpretability is one of the bottlenecks in NLP.
5. Context-aware language understanding and multi-turn dialogue systems will see breakthroughs. With the progress of technology and more data available, discourse understanding and open-domain dialogue systems are expected to advance further.
6. Cross-modal understanding and generation will progress further as the development of deep learning has made it possible to represent multi-modal information in the same space, and more cross-modal applications have provided massive amounts of data.

4.3 Industry Application Focus

Technology and application are promoting each other and advancing together. The progress of technology brings more applications, while more applications further drive the technology progress. As for NLP, it will be applied more widely in the following scenarios.

Chat-bots: General-purpose chat-bots for chit-chat and question answering will accelerate the development of smart home solutions and become more intelligent, capable of solving more problems, while domain-specific chat-bots will have increasing penetration rates in e-commerce, healthcare, finance, and other industries.

Virtual Assistant: Virtual assistants can help clients improve business processes, reduce costs, and raise their brand reputation.

Finance Industry: Constructing financial knowledge graphs by integrating massive amounts of financial data. Improving operational efficiency by means of public opinion monitoring, risk control, investment assistance, and news understanding.

Expert System Plus Healthcare/Law: Helping doctors and judges make decisions through the cross-modal understanding of medical or lawsuit cases, papers or files, and data from other sources.

Intelligent Writing Plus Media: Automatic writing or AI assisted writing can help in every step of media content production.

Sentiment Analysis: It can be used to provide marketing and competition information, increase client retention, or analyze the influence of events.

References

1. Wallace R. A.L.I.C.E. 2001. [Online]. Available: https://www.chatbots.org/chatterbot/a.l.i.c.e/.
2. Stanford University. SHRDLU. [Online]. Available: http://hci.stanford.edu/~winograd/shrdlu/.
3. Johnson J, Hariharan B, et al. CLEVR: a diagnostic dataset for compositional language and elementary visual reasoning. In: 2017 IEEE Conference on Computer Vision and Pattern Recognition (CVPR). 2017. p. 1988–1997.
4. Brown P, Della PS, Della PV, et al. The mathematics of machine translation: parameter estimation. Comput Linguist. 1993;19(2):263–311.
5. Wang H, Wu H, Liu Z. Word alignment for languages with scarce resources using bilingual corpora of other language pairs. In: Proceedings of the COLING/ACL-2006. 2006. p. 874–881.
6. Vaswani A, Shazeer N, Parmar N, et al. Attention is all you need. Adv Neural Inf Proces Syst. 2017;30:5998–6008.
7. Devlin J, Chang W, Lee K, et al. BERT: Pre-training of Deep Bidirectional Transformers for Language Understanding. In: Proceedings of the 2019 Conference of the North American Chapter of the Association for Computational Linguistics, Minnesota. 2019. p. 4171–4186.
8. Sun Y, Wang S, Li Y, et al. ERNIE 2.0: A Continual Pre-training Framework for Language Understanding. In: Proceedings of the Thirty-Fourth AAAI Conference on Artificial Intelligence. 2020.
9. ACL. Conference acceptance rates. [Online]. Available: https://aclweb.org/aclwiki/Conference_acceptance_rates.
10. Stanford. Artificial Intelligence Index 2019 Annual Report. December 2019.
11. WIPO. WIPO Technology Trends 2019: Artificial Intelligence, January 2019.
12. Tsinghua University Joint Research Center for Knowledge Intelligence. 2019 Artificial Intelligence Development Report, December 2019.
13. IDC. The Digitization of the World - From Edge to Core. November 2018.
14. Wang H, Yu S. The development of deep learning technologies. Research on the development of Electronic Information Engineering Technology in China. Beijing: Science Press; 2019.
15. Mordor Intelligence. Natural Language Progressing Market - Growth, Trends, and Forecast (2020–2025). 2019.
16. Watkins D. Global smart speaker vendor & OS shipment and Installed Base market share by region: Q4 2019. Boston: Strategy Analytics; 2020.
17. The State Council. New Generation Artificial Intelligence Development Plan, July 8, 2017.
18. Sun Y, Wang S, Li Y, et al. ERNIE: Enhanced representation through knowledge integration. arXiv preprint arXiv:1904.09223. 2019.

19. ASKCI Consulting. 2019 China Inbound and Outbound Tourism Data Analysis: International Tourism Revenue Reaches 131.3 billion US Dollars. 2020. [Online]. Available: https://baijiahao.baidu.com/s?id=1661403443466154048.

20. Chen C, Low J, et al. Canalys: Global smart speaker market to grow 13% in 2020 despite coronavirus disruption. Singapore: Canalys; 2020.

21. Wang H, Li Y, Wu T. Research and Applications of Large-scale Knowledge Graph. Commun CCF. 2018;14(1):47–53.

22. Socher R, Chen D, Manning CD, et al. Reasoning with neural tensor networks for knowledge base completion. In: Advances in neural information processing systems. MIT Press: Cambridge; 2013. p. 926–34.

23. Li F, Peng W, Chen Y, et al. Event extraction as multi-turn question answering. In: Findings of the Association for Computational Linguistics: EMNLP; 2020. p. 829–38.

24. Chen Q, Zhu X, Ling Z, et al. Neural natural language inference models enhanced with external knowledge. In: Proceedings of the 56th Annual Meeting of the Association for Computational Linguistics. 2018. p. 2406–2417.

25. Yang A, Wang Q, Liu J, et al. Enhancing pre-trained language representations with rich knowledge for machine reading comprehension. In: Proceedings of the 57th Annual Meeting of the Association for Computational Linguistics. 2019. p. 2346–2357.

26. Gao X. The construction of map of legal knowledge in application of artificial intelligence in civil justice: on the basis of essential facts theory. In: Law and social development; 2018. p. 66–80.

27. SemEval-2020 Task 9. [Online]. Available: https://competitions.codalab.org/competitions/20654#results. SemEval-2020 Task10. [Online]. Availabel: https://competitions.codalab.org/competitions/20815#results. SemEval-2020 Task12. [Online]. Available: https://sites.google.com/site/offensevalsharedtask/results-and-paper-submission.

28. SemEval-2016 Task 9. [Online]. Available: http://alt.qcri.org/semeval2016/task9/.

29. Xiao D, Zhang H, Li Y, et al. ERNIE-GEN: an enhanced multi-flow pre-training and fine-tuning framework for natural language generation. arXiv preprint arXiv:2001.11314v3. 2020.

30. Huang P, He X, Gao J, et al. Learning deep structured semantic models for web search using clickthrough data. In: Proceedings of the 22nd ACM International Conference on Information & Knowledge Management. 2013. p. 2333–2338.

31. Hu B, Lu Z, Li H, et al. Convolutional neural network architectures for matching natural language sentences. In: Advances in neural information processing systems. Cambridge: MIT Press; 2014. p. 2042–50.

32. Pang L, Lan Y, Guo J, et al. A Study of MatchPyramid Models on Ad-hoc Retrieval. arXive: 1606.04648. 2016.

33. Wan S, Lan Y, Xu J, et al. Match-srnn: Modeling the recursive matching structure with spatial rnn. arXiv preprint arXiv:1604.04378. 2016.

34. Sharing of big coffee Baidu semantic technology and full understanding of its application. Develop paper. 2019. [Online]. Available: https://www.programmersought.com/article/22681709645.

35. Zheng C, Sun Y, Wan S, et al. RLTM: an efficient neural IR framework for long documents. arXiv preprint arXiv:1906.09404. 2019.

36. Wang J, Huang P, Zhao H, et al. Billion-scale commodity embedding for e-commerce recommendation in alibaba. In: Proceedings of the 24th ACM SIGKDD International Conference on Knowledge Discovery & Data Mining. 2018. p. 839–848.

37. Zhang H, Wang S, Zhang K, et al. Towards Personalized and Semantic Retrieval: An End-to-EndSolution for E-commerce Search via Embedding Learning. arXiv preprint arXiv:2006.02282. 2020.

38. Wang Y, Liu K, Liu J, et al. Multi-Passage Machine Reading Comprehension with Cross-Passage Answer Verification. In: Proceedings of the 56th Annual Meeting of the Association for Computational Linguistics. 2018. p. 1918–1927.

39. Li H, Zhang X, Liu Y, et al. D-NET: A Pre-Training and Fine-Tuning Framework for Improving the Generalization of Machine Reading Comprehension. In: Proceedings of the 2nd Workshop on Machine Reading for Question Answering. 2019. p. 212–219.

40. Baidu Q. Financial Report: High Growth of Baidu APP, DAU Reaches 220 Million. 2020. [Online]. Available: http://news.iresearch.cn/yx/2020/05/323979.shtml.

41. Wang H, Wu H, Tian H, et al. AI-oriented Human Machine Interaction Method and System. China, 201510563338.2, 2015-09-07.

42. Bahdanau D, Cho K, Bengio Y. Neural Machine Translation by Jointly Learning to Align and Translate. arXiv:1409.0473. 2014.

43. Sutskever I, Vinyals O, et al. Sequence to Sequence Learning with Neural Networks. Adv Neural Inf Proces Syst. 2014;27:3104–12.

44. He W, He Z, Wu H, et al. Improved Neural Machine Translation with SMT Features. In: Proceedings of the Thirtieth AAAI Conference on Artificial Intelligence (AAAI 16). 2016. p. 151–157.

45. Xiong H, Zhang R, Zhang C, et al. DuTongChuan: Context-aware Translation Model for Simultaneous Interpreting. arXiv:1907.12984. 2019.

46. Dong D, Wu H, He W, et al. Multi-Task Learning for Multiple Language Translation. In: Proceedings of the 53rd Annual Meeting of the Association for Computational Linguistics and the 7th International Joint Conference on Natural Language Processing. 2015. p. 1723–1732.

47. Geng R, Li B, Li R, et al. Few-Shot Text Classification with Induction Network. arXiv preprint arXiv:1902.10482. 2019.

48. Yu M, Guo X, Yi J, et al. Diverse few-shot text classification with multiple metrics. arXiv preprint arXiv:1805.07513. 2018.

49. Wei J, Zou K. EDA: Easy Data Augmentation Techniques for Boosting Performance on Text Classification Tasks. In: Proceedings of the 2019 Conference on Empirical Methods in Natural Language Processing and the 9th International Joint Conference on Natural Language Processing. 2019. p. 6383–6389.

50. Yoo K, Shin Y, Lee S. Data augmentation for spoken language understanding via joint variational generation. In: Proceedings of the AAAI Conference on Artificial Intelligence. vol. 33. 2019. p. 7402-7409, .

51. Weizenbaum J. ELIZA - A Computer Program for the Study of Natural Language Communication Between Man and Machine. Communication of ACM. 1966;9(1):36–45.

52. Zhou X, Li L, Dong D, et al. Multi-turn Response Selection for Chatbots with Deep Attention Matching Network. In: Proceedings of the 56th Annual Meeting of the Association for Computational Linguistics. 2018. p. 1118–1127.

53. Zhou H, Young T, Huang M, et al. Commonsense Knowledge Aware Conversation Generation with Graph Attention. In: Proceedings of IJCAI. 2018. p. 4623–4629.

54. Liu Z, Niu Z, Wu Z, et al. Knowledge Aware Conversation Generation with Explainable Reasoning over Augmented Graphs. In: Proceedings of EMNLP-IJCNLP. 2019. p. 1782–1792.

55. Zhao T, Lee K, Eskénazi M. Unsupervised discrete sentence representation learning for interpretable neural dialog generation. In: Proceedings of ACL; 2018.

56. Zhao T, Xie K, Eskenazi M. Rethinking action spaces for reinforcement learning in end-to-end dialog agents with latent variable models. In: Proceedings of NAACL; 2019.

57. Kang D, Balakrishnan A, Shah P, et al. Recommendation as a communication game: self-supervised bot-play for goal-oriented dialogue. In: Proceedings of EMNLP; 2019.

58. Xu J, Wang H, Niu Z, et al. Knowledge Grasph Grounded Goal Planning for Open-domain Conversation Generation. In: Proceedings of AAAI; 2020.

Printed in the United States
by Baker & Taylor Publisher Services